Gá Gasced an 35ú Rang

Gá Gasced an 35ú Rang

What deeds, the 35th?

Compiled by Desmond Travers
Edited by Jane Travers

First edition September 2021

ISBN: 979-8-4627-9865-8

Independently published

Contents

Featured Photographs

35ú Rang Daltaí

Seasca Bliain ag Fás

Foreword by John Martin

Tuesday, the 31st of January 1961 was a cold and overcast day in the Curragh Camp. This was the background to the inauguration of the 35th Cadet Class or 35ú Rang Daltaí. The individuals who formed the Class were literally drawn from the four corners of Ireland, from Cork to Donegal and from Galway to Dublin, and many places in between. After eighteen months of gruelling and intensive training, the Class was commissioned on the square of Pearse Barracks in July 1962.

The individual members went their separate ways, and the 35th Cadet Class no longer existed as an entity in itself, but it remained a strong resonating memory for those who had been part of it. Sixty years later this production is an eclectic collection which chronicles the experiences, exploits and adventures of the members of the Class, both in military service and in the field of civilian endeavour.

The concept of the book came about as a consequence of a meeting in the Ashling Hotel in January 2020 BC (before Covid). The response to a request for material met with an enthusiastic reaction, and inputs by Class members have been varied and impressive. The combined work comprises recollections of service at home and abroad, travels and journeys since retirement, poetry, fiction and much more besides.

A special mention must be made of the contributions submitted by the families of deceased members, who entered into support for the project with enthusiasm. In this context mention must be made of Neil Taylor, Lynda Cooke, Claire Hartnett, Frances and Lucy Dodd and Ann Cotter. Out of the contacts made, a sort of social club has emerged through a

WhatsApp group. A primary characteristic of this group is the contribution it makes to the merriment quotient through the medium of funny stories and humorous cartoons. Appreciation is also deserved by those wonderful spouses who, working in the background, encouraged their husbands to write more flattering accounts of themselves than they might otherwise do.

Thanks also to those members of the Class, who in addition to making their contribution, submitted photos, press cuttings and assorted memorabilia which served to enhance the production. In particular thanks goes to George Kirwan, Paddy Walshe, Joe Fallon, Leo Brownen and Johnny Murray.

Above all, special and sincere appreciation is merited by the moving force behind the project. Des Travers demonstrated his excellent qualities of determination, persuasion, and patience in his efforts to coordinate diversity and drive the effort to completion.

In addition to the contributions of Class members three family members, offspring of Class members, were 'volunteered' to take in hand the challenges of editing, compilation, graphical representation and other tricky bits. Jane Travers fulfilled the role of editor, and graphic design work by further family members was also very kindly donated.

An Cosantóir and an officers association have expressed an interest in reproducing articles from this production. They will, of course, have to secure authors' approval in all instances.

This has been a tremendous accomplishment in bringing all the disparate aspects of the project together. It truly reflects the very essence of the spirit of members of 35ú Rang which remains undimmed despite the passage of years.

Seán T. Ó'Máirtín
Íar Dalta.

Editor's Note

Jane Travers

When Des first told me that he was compiling a book to celebrate his Cadet Class and asked me to help, I envisaged something along the lines of a pamphlet; a few pages of A4 stapled at the corners and posted out to those who wanted it. Imagine my surprise when the submissions began pouring in; poems, photographs, anecdotes and memories. What impressed and astonished me was not so much the army memories — I'm an army brat, I've heard them all — but the tales of classmates' adventures after their army life. The wealth and breadth of knowledge and experience gained in second careers astonishes me, and I am in awe of everyone's willingness to retrain and study, to travel and have new experiences. Over time as the book began to take shape, I started to recognise what a truly lovely thing is being created here, something that I hope will be cherished by classmates and their families for many years to come. I am proud to have played a small part in it.

I would also like to thank those people who have graciously and anonymously donated their time and skills to produce the high-quality graphics that you see throughout the book. We couldn't have done it without them. To them, a big thank you.

Paddy Walshe and Photo Processing Ltd, Newbridge were hugely supportive and helpful, and their work manifests itself here and there especially in the presentation and panel displays on the day of our gathering in the Cadet School.

I must not ignore our outsider friends who assisted us with this enterprise. They are:

Sean Curtis of Professional Tactical Equipment Ltd., www.protac.ie for advice, assistance and procurement of the final Ga Gasca 35ú Rang Challenge Coin.

Nicky Quinlan of Druid Craft, www.druidcraft.com and www.militarygiftsireland.com for advice on display and presentational work with challenge coins.

To them also a big thank you.

Jane Travers

Biography of Jane Travers

Jane Travers holds a BA in English and an MA in Film Studies, as well as a certificate in screenwriting. She has over ten years of experience in writing for publication, and she offers various document services on a freelance basis. These include transcription, research/fact-checking, proof-reading, editing and script-writing. She lives in Essex with her husband, daughter and two dogs.

Gá Gasced An 35á Rang

1961 - 2021

A Love Affair with Italy

Leo Brownen

At some stage in people's lives they reach a fork in the road which changes the whole course of their lives. Being unable to take a Battalion overseas in Autumn 1992, for serious family reasons, I was subsequently offered the appointment of Senior Ops Offs Officer in Naqoura. This position, which I readily accepted, was for a year, commencing in April 1993. This was the fork in the road which changed my life (and my wife's) and started our extraterritorial 'love affair' with Italy.

As Senior Operations Officer the helicopter unit called Italair came very much into my operational taskings on a daily basis. I had a little Italian from membership of a language/cultural group in Cork called 'The Dante Alighieri Society'. With the exception of their Ops Offr, Lt-Col Franco Gori, none of the Italair unit spoke English. However, a strong friendship developed from working with them and at their request I translated and edited their SOPs into more appropriate military terminology. Thereafter I concentrated on improving their reaction times in medical emergency situations and similarly retraining the Polish medical teams. Eventually we were able to get the completely outfitted and staffed Medevac Heli team into the air in 6 minutes. Other positive agreements by the Force Commander enabled the Ops Section to broaden and enhance the Italair role and make their service more widespread and more meaningful. In particular we installed night landing facilities in a third of all Unifil OPs so that all troops were within easy reach of a Medevac rescue team.

My new friend Franco in Italair subsequently invited my wife Anne and myself to spend a holiday in Italy with him and his family, in their beautiful villa 80 kms north of Venice, at the foot of the Dolomite

Mountains. The limitations of our respective communicative abilities did nothing to spoil the holiday but both parties agreed to study the other's language, to improve our interactive prospects. We took up the challenge and so the 'love affair' began. Some years later and after several reciprocate and enjoyable visits in Ireland and Italy I decided, on retirement in 2001, to study the language more seriously. Having already a BA Degree plus an H Dip in Education I was permitted to take the degree course in UCC as a single subject. This took 3 years of hard work but I succeeded in getting a 2.1 qualification, which I followed up with another year's course in Italian films and film making. Anne and I went on a month's immersion course thereafter, to a small Italian town in middle Italy, and we are now fairly proficient at the language.

I taught beginner's Italian in the Dante Society for two years, 2007/8, was subsequently elected on to the committee and have been the chairman for some 10 years now. Our society teaches Italian language and culture in a local school premises every Monday night from 7–9pm. We have between 80–100 members, employ three qualified native Italian teachers and have a wonderfully vibrant linguistic and social grouping.

In the intervening years we have travelled all over Italy on holidays and know it very well, plus its tragic history. Our friendship with Franco (subsequently Brig-Gen) and his family has strengthened over the years and we now regard them as part of our family.

We find the Italian people much like ourselves, friendly, sociable, great for partying, intensely loyal and willing to help the stranger. Their cooking abilities are renowned of course and they absolutely understand people who have special dietary requirements and make ample provision for them in restaurants and hotels.

Their music, literature and poetry is wonderful and if you ever have time for study read Dante's Divine Comedy (really means Drama). It is the finest and most engaging book I have ever read in my life. The 'love affair' continues and we are still hugely involved with all things Italian here in Cork and with our expanding group of friends in Italy. Retirement to sit and do nothing is not part of our agenda! Our lives have been greatly enhanced by that fork in the road and we rejoice that our decision in this respect worked out so well. We made lifelong friends and had great experiences. Try it!

Cari compagni, vi auguro buona salute e buona fortuna a tutti voi!

**Leo and Anne (in white blouse) with the Gori family
at their villa at the foot of the Dolomites.**

'Elvis Has Left the Building'

Patrick Laurence Cooke (Larry) (1941–2011)

By Lynda Archer (née Cooke)

Growing up, I was extremely proud of the fact that many of my school friends thought my Dad was a dead ringer for the 'King' himself. It makes me laugh now of course, but I basked in the reflected glory of that association. My Dad looked like Elvis!! I could see it in his quiff alright. But I'm not so sure that Elvis had ears like the handles of the Sam Maguire Cup!

Elvis, I'm sad to say, has now well and truly left the building. Taking with him his trademark quiff, a never-ending supply of iced-caramel sweets, a pint or three of Guinness, a medium rare steak, some onion rings and a generous helping of crème caramel!

I thought that this would be an easy task. That I would write an official account of my Father's career: talk up his achievements, reference his love of sports and maybe throw in a little known fact about him that might make you all smile. Like the fact that he was an Altar boy, or that he played the violin. That he wholeheartedly believed that he was *the* nattiest dresser on the planet, and the coolest dancer alive. Or that he owned *the* most magical pair of rose-tinted glasses any man could ever own *(but more on that later)*. Job done!

Instead I sit down to write, following what's turned out to be an emotional few days — humbled, immensely proud, a little cross with him if I'm honest; and very sad that it's taken an anniversary such as this for me to realise that one's parents *are* actually people — people who had lives long before I came along. And unless you ask about them, hear their stories and *really* find out — can you ever really know them?

I've spoken instead to aunts & uncles, neighbours and friends, my wonderful stepmother Carol and one or two of his class who would have known 'The Cooker' in a way I never knew.

He left no typed CV to refer to (though I am eternally grateful to the Cavalry Club for the biography supplied upon his death, which forms the backbone of the detail I *can* supply, certain in the knowledge that it is accurate).

"Focus on the later years, tell us about his UN-NY career," Des advised. "Fill in the gaps ... paint a picture of your Dad." I only hope I can. Dad was off in New York doing his thing. I was in London doing mine. We spoke — of course we did. But we never got into the 'detail'.

I have been told by many that he had real honour and that he was honest to a fault. That he had 'integrity in spades'. He was extremely articulate (when he wanted to be) and highly intelligent. He really didn't suffer fools gladly at all. Ever! He would 'cut the head off you' if he thought you weren't doing your best or telling him the truth, and he had an uncanny ability to cut through the waffle to get to the nub of any problem in minutes.

Of course, his particular way with words and his 'college major' in sheer bloody-mindedness meant that he didn't always deliver his point in the most diplomatic of ways. But by God he was (most annoyingly) very nearly always right! And apologise? Forget it!! Not even when it was he who accidently broke the news to me at the dinner table that there was no such a person as Santa. To be honest — the horror on his face when he realised what he'd said was enough of an apology in that instance!

He was also immensely witty, and an accomplished raconteur. He held court on many a night out and hung me out to dry on my wedding day — but it was all done in jest! Actually I realise now that it was his way of conveying real sentiment when mushy words would never do! He was 'army' after all. He would turn many a mundane scene into one of hilarity just by telling it how it was and delivering an observation that the rest of us were thinking but didn't dare to say out loud.

Dad had a particularly high opinion of his own sartorial elegance. The shirt always had to compliment the v-necked sweater. I never saw him wear a pair of jeans in my life (but he did sport what I would call Farah 'man trousers' ... even when tinkering in his shed!) And those rose-tinted glasses I mentioned earlier? Well, they came in particularly handy when overlooking the straining button or two over the years. It was always one of us who had shrunk his shirts in the wash! And that hair wasn't greying. We were the ones who needed glasses!

He had a particular turn of phrase that I came to associate with him given that I was the recipient so many times over the years: "Listen, an ff-ing monkey with a hammer up its a.. could do that!" Well, if the monkey could do it — whilst in such pain — then I knew that the same was expected of me!

He was also an incredibly kind man. He would literally do anything for anyone. Woe-be-tide you if you short changed him a penny on a restaurant bill; but you can be guaranteed that he would always give that same last penny to those less fortunate than himself. Always. That kindness extended too, to spending many a night well pickled because he'd been plied with our neighbour's lethal homemade wine. He could never ever have told him he hated the stuff — it just wouldn't be right.

There wasn't very much that scared my Dad. But he had a very real and pathological fear of hospitals which meant that he would let his rugby injuries go rather than have knee surgery, impacting his ability to walk properly in later years. This fear stopped him too, from visiting sick friends, old colleagues and family in hospital over the years. He literally couldn't step inside the front doors of a hospital, for anyone.

He lived for rugby. With his Curragh playing days behind him he became widely known in sporting circles as a rugby referee. In fact he continued to referee well into his 50s while living in New York, and attended weekly rugby referee meetings back home in Cork right up until he got sick. He was also a keen golfer though he didn't play much in his last years thanks to that old rugby knee injury.

I'm told by many that he would probably have been a builder or an architect had he not gone into the army. That love and appreciation for architecture never ever left him. He bought a 'doer-upper' to rebuild upon his retirement in 2004, which he managed while renovating the family home at the same time, often travelling between the two to the detriment of sleep. And he was forever stopping to admire buildings everywhere he went.

What I can attest to is his immense happiness in later years, and his real love affair with New York. He took to 'big city' life with aplomb, refereeing rugby games, playing golf and travelling the length and breadth of the States. He spoke to everyone, wherever they came from and was highly thought of by UN colleagues and friends alike. A 'creature of habit', prior to going there I would have told you he'd never stick it out; but he loved New York very much and it surely loved him.

He never did get to retire by the sea, which had always been his dream. He passed away on August 5th 2011, at the Bons Secours hospital, Cork with family by his side. He died of non-Hodgkin's Lymphoma, aged 69. He is survived by a daughter Lynda, who married to a New Zealander and is living in the UK with 2 children (1 girl, 1 rugby-mad boy), and a son Ronan who owns a restaurant and bar in Queens, New York, aptly called Saints 'n' Sinners! Ronan is married to an Irish girl and they have 2 beautiful boys, both of whom play ice-hockey. And let me pay a warm and heartfelt tribute to my friend and his loving partner Carol who nursed him to the very end.

My closing words however go to you, the men of his 35th Cadet Class. He would have loved to be there with you, reminiscing, re-writing history, re-living the stories. I get the sense that lifelong bonds are forged in cadet class. It was in fact to members of this class that he turned in his last months. One of you got to say your goodbyes in person at the very end, on everyone's behalf. You know who you are and as a family we will always be eternally grateful for all the help you gave us.

Given all the lovely things I've been told about my Dad these past few days, I wish I could tell him how immensely proud I am to be a Cooke, to be his daughter. How lucky am I to know that I possess (she hopes) just a few of the character traits which were actually the very best of him.

And I gently implore you all to make a real and concerted effort to 'fill in' the gaps in your own family's knowledge right now. Tell them about your career, tell them all about yourself, the decisions you've made. The paths never taken. The person you were in the beginning, the person you are today. Tell them how it was and how it is. Do not leave it till it's too late.

For in the words of George Elliot, "Our dead will never be dead to us until we have forgotten them." My Dad is a hard man to forget and I salute him.

With love and much admiration for you all.

Lynda Archer (née Cooke)

A Brief Résumé

- Born on November 4th 1941, my father was raised in Turners Cross, Cork City. The third of 5 children and the son of a Police Sergeant and a Domestic Economy teacher, he attended Coláiste Chríost Rí.

- He joined the Army as a member of the 35th Cadet Class in January 1961.

- Commissioned in July 1962, he worked first as a Recce Troop Commander with the 4th Motor Squadron in Plunkett Barracks, Curragh Camp.

- During his service, he held a wide range of appointments in the Corps and outside, including School Commandant Cavalry School, Squadron Commander 1st Armoured Car Squadron, Officer in Charge Cavalry Workshops, Operations Officer Curragh Command, School Commandant NCO School General Training Depot, Kildare Regional Civil Defence Officer and Staff Officer, and Staff Officer Observer Corps.

- He first worked overseas in 1963 with the Armoured Car Group, 39th Infantry Battalion (ONUC).

- In 1966 he was Technical Officer with the Armoured Car Group, 7th Infantry Group (UNFICYP).

- He then spent 2 years in the Middle East as a Military Observer with UNTSO in 1970–1972 and upon his return, attended the Bolton Street College of Technology where he completed a Motor Engineer Management course in 1972.

- He was well known throughout the Corps and throughout the Defence Forces from his time in Cavalry Workshops, first as the Technical Officer (July 1973 to May 1977) and then as OIC Workshops (August 1978 to April 1985). He then became a Logistics Officer with the 59th Infantry Battalion (UNIFIL) in 1986.

- In later years, he worked in the Department of Peacekeeping Operations at UN Headquarters, New York from August 1995, until his retirement as Lieutenant Colonel, from the Defence Forces in May 1999; during which time I understand that he was awarded The United Nations Medal in recognition of his service.

- He continued to work there in a civilian capacity until his final retirement in 2004 and although I am unable to give an accurate chronological breakdown of his time in New York I remember that he worked for long periods of time in Rwanda, in Angola, in Haiti and in East Timor.

Frank: Soldier, Philosopher, Husband, Father

Francis Dominick Cotter (1942–2002)

By Ann Cotter

Ann and Frank in their garden in Waterlooville

When Frank left the Irish Army in 1967 he took up a 3 year contract with the Zambian Police Department. Whilst there in 1968 he met me. I was also on a 3 year contract working as a secretary for the Zambian Ministry of Labour. We married within a few months of meeting and in July 1969 our first son Brian was born.

Kevin, Brian and Annette in Bangkok, Oct 2010

When his contract expired in May 1970 we flew home and stayed with my parents in Portsmouth, in the UK. We bought a cottage just outside Portsmouth in Waterlooville and with an expanding family (Annette born in 1971 and Kevin in 1974) moved a short distance to a larger house, where we stayed and where sadly in 2002 at the age of 60, Frank passed away, as a result of liver cancer.

Frank had done a couple of jobs before he was employed in 1975 by McMurdo Engineering in Portsmouth as an inspector. He rose to Quality Control Manager and was still employed by them when he died in September 2002. They had been amazing employers all the way through his years with cancer, which he was diagnosed with in 1997.

Frank's passion was drawing and painting and a little bit of writing too. I have boxes of his sketchbooks. He never ventured out without his sketchbook. He wrote a very funny short story/manual when he was in the Army entitled The Reserve of Men. I think some of his friends from that time may remember it. He loved walking and many of our holidays were spent walking various long distance footpaths and bridleways across the UK, initially with small children in tow and eventually just the two of us. He also loved his garden and at one time we had 2 allotments on the go, filling the freezer with fruit and veg.

I feel privileged to have met this intellectual, well read, interesting man and we all still miss him every single day.

Frank and Ann Cotter with their son Brian,
and Paddy and Carmel Walshe.

Extract from 'The Reserve of Men'
(unpublished)

Frank Cotter

Section 1 — Preamble and Definition

1. The Reserve of Men: The Reserve of Men (hereinafter known as the ROM), a force permanently established on a part-time basis, an elite body of men which at all times hold itself in readiness to assist His Excellency The Civil Administrator in His various activities in the environments and townlands of Ireland and places abroad.

2. The Brigadier: In the ROM there will be one Brigadier who will be known as The Brigadier.

3. Grades of Rank: THE ROM will have two grades of Officer rank — Colonel and Captain. Other Ranks (hereinafter known as ORs) will be graded as follows: Man and Private Man — the former will be superior to the latter.

4. Establishment: The strength of the ROM will be set in accordance with the requirements of the situation or which may obtain at any particular time but will never exceed twenty three Officers and ORs at any time.

5. Jurisdiction: THE ROM will be under the jurisdiction of His Excellency, The Civil Administrator who may or may not issue, from time to time, directives for the guidance and edification of The Brigadier.

6. Control: THE ROM will at all times come under the direct control of The Brigadier; all orders on any issue will emanate from The Brigadier and the management and conduct of both tactical and strategic operations will be entirely at his discretion.

7. The Drill: The Drill will be strictly adhered to by all Officers and ORs of the ROM; all activities of the ROM to be carried out in accordance with The Drill.

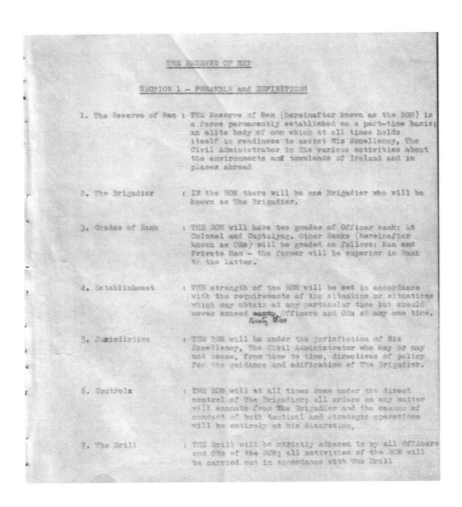

Extract from Frank's original manuscript

Carl: Soldier, Husband, Father

Carl Dodd (1942–2018)

By Frances and Lucy Dodd

Dad would have relished writing this article. He would have taken his time mulling over the personal reflections he wanted to share, and then spent many hours rewriting it over and over again using his fountain pen, until he was totally happy with it. Dad was a great storyteller, unfortunately this skill didn't pass down to me!

Dad always maintained that he was very lucky to be offered a cadetship, as he didn't know what would have become of himself otherwise. I think that the army also lucked out with the 35th Cadet Class, and benefited tremendously from your collective leadership, innovations & hard work!

Neither Mam nor I can recall any stories about his own personal experiences as a cadet, but we are pretty confident that Doddy was in the middle of, or the initiator of the odd bit of craic! We suspect that his 'Mulligans Motor Bike' party piece was belted out every now and again. What is abundantly clear is that you all formed a unique bond during your time in the Cadet School that has never broken as you are still looking out for each other! I always knew when one of you had come to visit Dad in the hospital or at home even before he told me about his day. He was always recharged and re-energized from your conversations. Mam and I will always be grateful to you for your kindness.

Dad's first appointment luckily was to the 12th Battalion in Clonmel training recruits, as it was there that he met Mam when they were both set up on a blind date. At the tender age of 21 Dad headed off on his first UN assignment with the 40th Infantry Battalion to Cyprus. There is a short RTE news archive video of the parade prior to their departure, and you can see Dad in the footage: https://bit.ly/3mm5NSm. As soon as he got back Mam and Dad got married. The remainder and the majority of Dad's army career was then either based in the Curragh, Dublin or abroad.

I found Dad's Trinity application for his Master's in Political Science, and it included a detailed year by year listing of his various appointments and courses undertaken. It was impressive and akin to a CEO and University Provost all tied into one. I totted up that Dad spent about sixteen years either engaged in providing training courses in all schools of the Military College or in charge of the schools. Teaching is in the Dodd genes and so he was playing to his strengths sharing his knowledge & experiences with the next generation. He was delighted to be appointed Commanding Officer of the Cadet School, Head of the Military College & General Officer Commanding Defence Forces Training Centre.

Like the rest of his cadet class peers over the course of his career Dad got lots of plaques & awards which are all carefully packed away in the press, together with all his army photos. It's revealing that there are only three military items or remembrances that he chose to display. They are all on the mantelpiece in the sitting room, where they still have pride of place — his award from the Advanced Infantry Course, a going away recognition from the Third Battalion and a picture from his final UN posting in Israel.

**Distinguished Allied Graduate
School of Infantry,
Fort Benning, Georgia:
Capt Carl Dodd, 1974**

There was just once during Dad's army career that we got the opportunity as a family to travel with him abroad. In 1974 we travelled to Fort Benning, Georgia where Dad was selected to attend the US Army Advanced Infantry Career Course. It was a fantastic opportunity for all of us! As you can imagine, Dad made friends quickly with both his US & allied peers. While he had fun, he was also very studious. He spent many hours every night and weekend at his desk in the bedroom studying. There were tons of manuals stacked up one on top of the other on the floor beside him. He was in his element, writing meticulous notes, puffing away on his pipe and relishing this great learning opportunity. All the hard work paid off as he was awarded the Top Allied Student. It was an outstanding achievement for him.

Dad got to spend six years of his career in various roles in the Third Battalion. However, there is no doubt that being appointed Officer Commanding the battalion was one of his top career highlights. It was what all his training and experiences up till that point had been leading to, and it was extra special to him that it was with his beloved 'bloods'.

You couldn't stop him talking at dinner time about his day: he loved it and he also gained personally from the experience. I also know from personal experience that he could be a hard task master when he felt it was needed. At least when it came to me, he was normally right! He wasn't afraid to make tough decisions, but what we experienced at home is that these tough decisions were not easy for him. He would mull them over and over in his head to ensure he was making the best decision.

In 1999, there were great celebrations in the house when Dad was promoted to Major General. He was appointed as Deputy Chief of Staff Operations and he was back up to Dublin. It was a tough challenging job with a very wide scope. It involved being able to navigate both civil & military relationships. As usual he gave it his best shot!

In 2002, after much discussion at home with Mam, Dad agreed to take the position of Chief of Staff UNTSO in 2002. He took this important peacekeeping role very seriously. He worked at it day and night for two and a half years till he retired. It was his most challenging role yet, commanding a multinational peacekeeping operation with officers for 24 different countries, international civilian staff, as well as local staff in each of the 5 countries. He put in a lot of air miles building and sustaining relationships with both the military and governments across the five countries. For a man who hated flying ever since he got his airborne wings in Fort Benning, that was no mean feat. Thankfully Mam was with him for the later part of his assignment. I also got to spend a few days in Government House with them both, when work also brought me to Israel. It was the Dad I remembered from the Third Battalion days, talking non-stop about his day during dinner. If there ever was a man suited to that job it was Dad! He was in his element! He had the experience needed to be successful and also his skill of being able to talk to anyone about anything was essential for this role. I am told that he even managed to impress the Israeli military authorities which is no mean feat, and the Lebanese Government awarded him the Order of the Cedar. Mam and I were so proud of him, but more importantly he was proud of himself.

Near the end of his military career Dad started going on the annual Army pilgrimage to Lourdes. He loved it so much he continued to go when he retired, for as long as he could. For him it was a joyful combination of all the things he held dear — the army, family, some prayer and the odd pint in the evening! He was so proud to be a member of the Irish army and there was always a twinkle in his eyes marching to mass behind the army pipers every day. If you haven't gone, you should consider it!

**Commander,
Order of the Cedar, Lebanon
Maj Gen Carl Dodd, 2006**

Dad absolutely loved the army. It was his great honour to serve his country and to play his role in supporting peace through the United Nations in Cyprus, Lebanon, Central America & UNTSO. He would have served for longer if he had been let! He admitted to it himself that retirement was initially hard for him, as he has been giving 150% in UNTSO right up to the very last day, and all of a sudden, his military career was over. But he soon got his head around it and focused on his love of learning and headed off to Trinity college to successfully complete his Master's in Political Science where his fellow students also gained from his army & UN experience. There is only one regret that Dad shared with me about his army career and that was the family life he missed out on during his combined seven years of UN service. We missed him terribly when he went away, but that was simply part and parcel of having a Dad in the army! I know he was very appreciative of Mam's support and keeping the show on the road back home.

While Dad always thought that he was lucky to join the army, the army was lucky to have benefited from both his and the rest of the 35th Cadet Class' hard work, dedication and family sacrifices over their military careers.

A Résumé

Major General Carl Dodd

By Frances and Lucy Dodd

Major General Carl Dodd was commissioned into the infantry corps in July 1962, in the rank of Second Lieutenant. His first posting was to the 12th Infantry Battalion in Clonmel, Co. Tipperary (Southern Command). Between commissioning and 1969 he spent most of his service in the 12th Infantry Battalion and as Training Officer with the 15th Infantry Battalion (Local Defense Forces) in County Kerry. In 1969 he was promoted to Captain and was posted to the Infantry School, Military College as an instructor. He spent most of his service as a Captain in the Infantry School until his promotion to Commandant in 1978 where he was posted as an instructor with the Command and Staff School. Between 1981 and 1984 he was posted as a Staff Officer in Training Section, Chief of Staff's branch. He subsequently served as a Company Commander and Battalion Second in Command with the 3rd Battalion, Curragh Command between 1985 and 1990. He was appointed Brigade Operations Officer with the 6th Brigade, Curragh in March 1991, before being appointed Staff Officer, Operations in Curragh Command HQ in September 1991. He was promoted Lieutenant Colonel in January 1992 and posted as Officer Commanding Third Infantry Battalion, Curragh. In January he was posted as School Commandant, The Cadet School, Military College. He was promoted to Colonel in April 1995 and posted as Director of Operations, Chief of Staff's Branch, Defense Forces HQ. In February 1998 he was promoted to Brigadier General and posted as Commandant, The Military College. In September 1999 he was promoted to Major General and posted as Deputy Chief of Staff (Operations), Defense Forces HQ.

United Nations Service

He served as Platoon Commander with the 40th Infantry Battalion (UNFICYP) in Cyprus 1964. In 1970/71 he served as Operations Officer of the 19th Infantry Group (UNFICYP) in Cyprus. In 1979 he was Company Commander of 'C' Company, 45 Infantry Battalion (UNIFIL) in Lebanon and in 1984/85 he was Senior Staff Officer in Operations Section at UNFICYP HQ in Nicosia, Cyprus. In 1990/91 he was posted as a Military Observer with ONUCA (Central America) and spent his service in Nicaragua.

Education

Major General Dodd is from Mallow, Co. Cork and before entering the Cadet School he attended the Patrician Academy in Mallow. He is a graduate of the Advanced Infantry Course in Fort Benning, Georgia, USA.

Marital Status

He is married to Frances and they have one daughter, Lucy, who was born in 1966. They live in Newbridge, Co. Kildare.

Interests

He is keenly interested in sport and in particular Gaelic Football. He is also a keen gundog enthusiast and regularly participates in Gundog (Springer Spaniel) Trials, game shooting and coursing.

Reminiscence

Eamon Draper

Eamon in The Riordans, 1971

Memory is a curious thing, that remembrance of things past that so often can catch you unawares. You may forget, but your memory never does. It just files things away to resurrect them whenever it will. No direct input from you is required: a piece of music, a scent, a place, a picture; these are the triggers, and suddenly the memory reveals itself.

Some time ago, looking for some book or other, I stood in front of the bookcase, somewhat curious as to what I had amassed over the years. A somewhat eclectic collection — history, military history; Sun Tzu, believe it or not; historical novels; thrillers; horror stories and so on.

Stuffed by category of course, are Poe's Complete Works, ditto Ray Bradbury, H.P. Lovecraft, Conan Doyle and James Michener. Works of reference: Bullfinch's Mythology and Brewer's Dictionary of Phrase and Fable. The Classics: King James Bible, The Odyssey, The Divine Comedy, the Bard of course, Dubliners and Ulysses.

Nestled snugly between Dylan Thomas' short stories and a complete Tennyson was a hardback copy of Patricia Lynch's The Turfcutter's Donkey hardback with Sean Keating's colour and black and white illustrations, bought some time ago, in a fit of nostalgia, in Charlie Byrne's famous Galway bookshop.

Some once upon a time memories are awakened, not in any orderly fashion as I am quite incapable of remembering anything in chronological order: writing an autobiography would be quite beyond me. The aforementioned donkey sparked a moment in time — Enid Blyton's Five and Seven; W.E. Johns' Biggles and Gimlet; Treasure Island and The Coral Island; The Dog Crusoe and the Wind in the Willows. I feel I am not alone with my memories of these. Others, millions I suppose, were enthralled by them too.

So there was Big Ears, along with Eileen, Seamus the leprechaun and the Yellow Tinker, neatly tucked up between Dylan and Alfred. In the company of Edgar Allan, Homer, Dante and James Joyce and a host of other well-loved stories.

At or about the time I read The Turfcutter's Donkey — I was ten years old — I had another 'first'. My first performance in a play (school plays are not to be so considered). A *real* play in a *real* theatre! This was on the stage of the Cork Opera House, or, as people of my vintage still refer to it, the 'old' Opera House. From the Abbey Theatre came Máire O'Donnell, Geoff Golden and Mícheál Ó h-Aonghusa to play in Dónal

Giltinan's The Goldfish in the Sun, a play set in Cork, the 'goldfish' of the title being the gold salmon on the top of Shandon Steeple.

O'h-Aonghusa and Golden were both from Cork, and Máire and Geoff had both recently married. Years later when I went to the Abbey, Máire remembered me from that time and both she and Geoff's brother Eddie were extremely kind to me as a (relatively) young actor at the National Theatre.

Before turning professional, Geoff had been a member of the Cork Shakespearean Company founded in 1926 by Fr O'Flynn. Called 'The Loft' affectionately by Cork people (because it was over a sweet factory) it produced many fine actors who went to play in theatres all over the world, as well as in film and TV. There was the aforementioned Geoff Golden and his brother Eddie, both noted Abbey actors; also Joe Lynch, Chris Curran, Kevin Flood and Edward Mulhare; the latter replaced Rex Harrison on Broadway in My Fair Lady and went on to subsequent TV fame in The Ghost and Mrs. Muir and Knight Rider. I myself was also a member of this illustrious company and sad to say I am the last man standing.

Fr O'Flynn was one of the most unforgettable people I've ever met and has had a profound influence on my life. His knowledge of Shakespeare and how to approach his plays was extensive. His diktat — "fit the words to the emotion, never the emotion to the words," has been my guide, not just with Shakespeare, but with many other playwrights and various scripts. Despite his fame (he was the subject of a BBC TV documentary), when asked how he would like to be remembered, he always said, "as a priest". In the public park in Passage West, across the road from the church where he was parish priest, and where he is buried, is a bust by the sculptor Séamus Murphy on the plinth of which is the simple inscription, 'Seamus O'Floinn, Saggart'.

Over the years I have directed many Shakespearean productions, including Verdi's Grand Opera Macbeth, in which he scrupulously adhered to both plot and text. This I directed for Taibhdhearc Na Gaillimhe, the National Irish Language Theatre.

While working on this production I had the following exchange in the street with a noted broadcaster and man of the theatre —

"I hear you're doing Macbeth."

" Yes."

"D'opera?"

"Yes."

"Verdi?"

"Yes."

"In Irish?"

"Yes."

"Ah, I wouldn't understand that at all."

"You wouldn't have understood it in Italian either."

Oh yes! Patricia Lynch. She was pushed to one side by thoughts and memories conjured up by the adventures of the turf cutter's children and their fantastic friends and the characters they met.

So! Patricia Lynch! I had the great privilege of meeting her once. It was at the Embankment in Tallaght, at that time an established venue for folk-music and the first 'pub theatre' which I and some colleagues began. Patricia and her journalist husband, Roy Fox, were attending a production of mine, which I cannot recollect. Following the performance I was introduced to her and had the good fortune to spend more than half an hour in her company, just the two of us in the corner of the bar room, with me 'listening to her and asking questions'. She told me that she had dreamt all her stories. Unforgettable, indeed inspirational, to meet a childhood idol.

So full circle, book to author. All stored, not in any chronological order, but in there; the voices, the thoughts, the feelings of days long gone encroaching on the mind in a random way, all mixed up like a jigsaw yet to be approached: meeting Maureen O'Hara; Canon Sydney McEwan ('Queen of the May') celebrating Mass for the opening of the Cork Film Festival in 1972, when it was in its heyday; the 'family' feel of the cast of The Riordans and a myriad other thoughts of the past retained, unforgotten, in the memory.

Also there is the cadet school which took up a solid chunk of our lives, meeting total strangers who became friends and with whom you form long-lasting friendships, though you may not get together that often. Also as Brian McManus (alas no longer with us) said to me, the cadet school leaves a mark on you that is entrenched and enduring, no matter to what you may subsequently turn your hand.

All this, or some of it at least, smacks of nostalgia and nostalgia is a thing of the past. And the past is a very foreign country, where apparently they do things differently.

Getting older does, I suppose, concentrate the mind to some extent. But then, as William Faulkner said, "The past is never dead. It's not even past".

Somehow I prefer Shakespeare's "Call back yesterday, bid time return". And I suppose that's about the best we can achieve at a certain stage in life. So — more reminiscing, less planning!

A Life in Theatre

Eamon Draper

I began with the Abbey and then most of the theatres in Dublin, not quite 'second spear-carrier from the left', but not exactly the guard-commander either! But one progresses surprisingly rapidly.

Then television, while still working in theatre, although theatre work was scarce enough in the early seventies. As a result, a few of us got together 'to make our own work', and so began the first pub-theatre in the country — we would go back to Shakespeare, Marlowe and Jonson, back to the inn yard!

Our first production was Behan's The Hostage at Mick McCarthy's Embankment in Tallaght, then a mile out in the country. Brendan's mother, Kathleen, was in the audience, as was his widow Beatrice. (Incidentally, Beatrice's father Cecil French-Salkeld painted the morning, noon and night murals in Davy Byrne's in Duke Street.) It was an amazing night, people seated at tables drinking and wrapped up in the play and there was quite a sing-song later in the bar, led by Kathleen.

I found myself directing all of the productions, while still performing on stage and TV. Among our productions was Synge's Playboy, Tom Murphy's Whistle in the Dark, Heno Magee's Hatchet and two of O'Casey's rising/war of independence/civil war trilogy, The Plough and the Stars and Shadow of a Gunman.

For Plough I approached the Dept of Defence for weapons, received permission and collected them from Johnny Murray who was stationed in Clancy Barracks at the time. I don't know whether he remembers that or not. At any rate, we had some of the weapons that were run in at

Howth, useful publicity of course. Our weapons were lodged in Tallaght Garda Station, collected and returned each evening. Very different times!

Over the years I have worked with Ulick O'Connor on his one-man shows on Behan and Gogarty. When Chris O'Neill, who was acting as his agent, first asked me to go with him to Letterkenny, I told him what was required was a stage manager not a director. His reply was, "I need someone to sit on him."

We travelled to Brussels at the invitation of our then commissioner Michael O'Kennedy. Chris also told me that any time he called Ulick to tell him he had a date for him, his first remark was, "Get me the Captain. I'm not going anywhere without the Captain."

Television and stage work continued in tandem, doing one or the other, sometimes both. My first lead on television was an adaptation of Jennifer Johnson's book The Gates where I played opposite Sorcha Cusack. What still amuses me about this is that I was playing an eighteen year old and I was thirty-two!

A variety of roles over the years after that. I have the doubtful distinction of having been in every 'soap' except Tolka Row, but that was before my time. In The Riordans I played Willie Maloney, 'the Mike Baldwin of Leestown', or, as I referred to him, "the resident shite!" In Fair City I played Aindrias Finnerty, an ex-army officer who may, or may not be, a con-artist. Turned out eventually that he couldn't go through with his scam! In Glenroe I was always available in court as the local district justice. In Ros Na Rún I played a retired doctor, father of the local GP. He misdiagnoses while standing in for his daughter. For TG4, I was in their four-part political drama The Running Mate and other programmes.

Eamon and Tom Hickey in The Riordans

I dubbed voices for Irish language versions of cartoons and live action programmes, including the voice of Dumbledore in the Harry Potter movies which still turn up every year around Christmas. Much else over the years, up to the latest Game of Thrones and Vikings.

My first time in Galway was when I was asked to direct Pinter's The Caretaker for Taibhdhearc Na Gaillimhe. This was supposed to take six weeks but I ended up in the 'city of tribes' for considerably longer. I was asked to direct their next play and given a choice of the play I would like to do. I chose John Arden's Sergeant Musgrave's Dance and also directed their next production, Tom Murphy's Famine. So my initial six weeks became almost a year, and began my love affair with this fantastic, almost magical city.

I worked mainly with An Taibhdhearc (I was artistic director there for four years), but also, for the first time, became involved in directing musicals, both with An Taibhdhearc and the Patrician Musical Society.

What, to me, is even more important, is that, had I remained in Dublin, I would never have been given an opportunity to direct Grand Opera. In Galway I was.

My first opera was Carmen, for the Patrician Musical Society, not one of my better efforts I have to admit. As I said to Patricia Lillis, the musical director, "You do realise I'm bringing forty years of ignorance to this?" But I'm a quick learner and worked with her on many other musicals.

I directed two further operas for An Taibhdhearc, Verdi's Rigoletto and Macbeth and still regard the Taibhdhearc production of Rigoletto as the best thing I have ever done, including my design for the sets. A member of the audience said one word to me on the opening night, "Éacht," a word for which there is no English equivalent. Composer Tom Cullivan texted the following day, "Bravo! Maestro!" A review for the Sunday Tribune, no longer with us, called it "...a triumph of artistic integrity over a shortage of funds." I subsequently directed Rigoletto again for the 50th anniversary of the Patrician Musical Society — English translation this time, not Irish.

We say in this business that you retire when you drop dead, but the bleak future from Covid 19 may very well have accelerated this. Time will tell.

So there you have it — *agus má tá bréag ann, bíoch!*

Coolmoney, Glen of Imaal, 1961
with Sergeant 'The Rua' O'Suilleabháin

1973 October War in the Middle East
[Extract from Green Cap and Blue Beret, published 2021]

Joe Fallon

From April 1973 I served as a UN Military Observer (UNMO) in the Middle East and was stationed with the UN control centre at Ismailia (ICC) which had a rear HQ in Cairo, where UNMOs and their families lived. Captains Barry Studdert (32nd cadet class) and Liam Gavin (34th cadet class) were also serving in ICC. On 6th October I was on OP duty on the west bank of the Suez Canal when the Egyptian 2nd and 3rd armies crossed into occupied Sinai and attacked Israel. Egypt's initial success ended ten days later when Israel counter-attacked, crossing the canal and penetrating deep into Egypt. A UN ceasefire, which was declared on 22nd October, was ignored by both sides but mainly by Israel. On 24th October I returned with Commandant Wolloch, OIC ICC, to Ismailia to re-establish our HQ. We had been forced to close it by the Egyptian authorities two weeks earlier as they had considered it was no longer necessary. Also on 24th October, seven teams of UNMOs from Cairo were dispatched to the front-lines, tasked with observing the non-effective ceasefire. The Soviet Union threatened to move troops to the canal zone to support the Egyptian army and the USA responded by going on world-wide nuclear alert. The UN Security Council established an Emergency Force (UNEF) and rushed troops overnight from nearby Cyprus to Egypt. Major General Siilasvuo COS UNTSO was appointed Force Commander UNEF and Colonel P D Hogan, Senior Staff Officer UNTSO, was appointed Chief of Staff UNEF which had its HQ in the UNTSO rear HQ Cairo.

I was recalled from Ismailia to UNEF HQ on the afternoon of 27th October to become an operations officer. UNEF HQ was staffed initially by UNTSO personnel. Colonel Hogan briefed me on my new role and as I had been without sleep for the previous eighty-four hours he told me to return to my home nearby and get a few hours sleep before reporting back on duty. Thirty minutes after arriving home, I was recalled by Colonel Hogan. He directed me to take an Egyptian military delegation to a location behind the Israeli lines near Suez City, for urgent talks with an Israeli delegation that night. The main issue for discussion was the resupply of the surrounded Egyptian 3rd Army with its 30,000 men and 300 tanks, located on the East bank of the Suez Canal. If permitted, I was to attend the meeting and file a report on my return to UNEF HQ. When I told Colonel Hogan that such a trip at night bordered on suicidal, he replied, "Have faith, young Fallon."

I was about to embark on a journey which would have a profound impact on my military career and would lead me to a range of extraordinary experiences over the following twenty-five months that I could never have envisaged when I left Athlone the previous April with my wife Marguerite and our two children, Joseph and Michele. My days of observing and reporting from an OP were over. Instead, I was about to become involved, initially in the negotiations between Egypt and Israel in Sinai and subsequently, those between Israel and Syria related to the Golan Heights. The negotiations were carried out in Egypt, Israel, Syria, Lebanon and Switzerland.

At 2000 hours on Saturday 27 October, I met with two Egyptian Officers outside UNEF HQ. One was General Gamasy, who I understood was the Director of Operations; in fact he had been Chief of Staff for the previous ten days. The second, much younger officer was Colonel Howeidi. The two officers got into my vehicle and the General told me we were going to Km109 which I knew was behind the Israeli FDLs. We drove slowly through a number of checkpoints near Cairo until we reached the open desert. As we approached Km 80 I was surprised that we did not appear to be moving through Egyptian positions but I kept my counsel. At Km 90 a group of Egyptian soldiers appeared out of the sand dunes close to the road and halted us and we were ordered out of the vehicle. The Lieutenant Colonel in charge recognised the General. His unit had been wiped out and he had only eight soldiers with him. The General directed him to establish a checkpoint and we drove on.

As we continued towards Km101, even with the limited light, I could see we were driving through a scene of devastation and carnage: burned-out trucks, tanks and APCs littered the road on both sides. We continued eastwards avoiding bomb craters, burnt-out vehicles and the bodies of a large number of Egyptian soldiers until we were halted by an Israeli patrol who escorted us to Km109 where we arrived at 2140. Our meeting place consisted of two Israeli APCs covered with camouflage netting. We were welcomed by General Yariv, a former Director of Intelligence, and by Colonel Sion who was married to Ruth Dyan the daughter of Moshe Dyan, the Israeli Defence Minister. Following coffee, both delegations sat down and I was not asked to leave.

General Yariv opened the meeting by stating that both sides had fought a hard and honourable war and must now move forward from that point. In the context of the humiliation suffered by Egypt at the hands of Israel in 1956 and 1967, I thought it was a significant opening remark. General Yariv wished to discuss: a) how a sound ceasefire could be maintained with both armies in such close proximity to each other, and b) the early release of their POWs. On the other hand, General Gamasy had two primary interests: a) Israel's return to the ceasefire lines of 22nd October when the 3rd Army or Suez City were not surrounded and b) the provision of resupplies for the 3rd Army and for Suez City. During the discussion which followed, it transpired that Israel, under pressure from the USA, had agreed to allow one convoy of food and water to be delivered to the 3rd Army only. The convoy would consist of 125 Egyptian lorries of food and water, driven by UN drivers who were being flown in from Cyprus. It was agreed that the convoy would go to the former UN OP Kilo on the west bank of the canal, which was now an Israeli strongpoint. Egyptian ferries and amphibious APCs would cross to the west bank and collect the supplies.

The meeting ended around midnight and we were escorted by the Israelis to Km 101. I continued on through the carnage, driving slowly with the vehicle doors ajar to facilitate a rapid exit. We arrived back at UNEF HQ at 0400 and the two Egyptian officers departed. I commenced preparation of minutes of the meeting. As both sets of delegates had spoken slowly, I had in effect, a verbatim account of the deliberations. My report was typed and when approved by General Siilasvuo, was forwarded to UN HQ New York.

I arrived home at 0730 and had started breakfast when an UNMO arrived and told me to report immediately to Colonel Hogan who briefed me on the latest problem. The Egyptian food convoy was heading towards Km101. As I was the only UN officer who understood what had been agreed the night before, I was directed to take command of the convoy and ensure that the supplies were delivered to the 3rd Army. The only transport that was available for me was a VW Variant with a faulty radio.

I departed for Km101 and was barely able to stay awake. I stopped at the checkpoint manned by the Lieutenant Colonel who now had twenty troops. I shared the fruit which I had with him and his troops and I continued to Km101 where the 125 supply trucks had been taken over by the UNEF drivers. My first task was to secure a working radio. I saw a fellow UNMO from Cairo sitting in a new UN vehicle and I approached him and told him I needed to exchange vehicles or radios. At first, he refused but eventually, he agreed.

I then approached the local Israeli commander who would not allow the convoy through as he 'had no instructions'. I told him that was nonsense as I had been with General Yariv the night before and he had assured the UN that his troops would be aware of the convoy's arrival. I advised him that I would contact UN New York to report his refusal, (despite the fact that I had difficulty contacting a fellow UNMO ten minutes earlier). The bluff worked and I led the convoy forward. At Km109 I was blocked again and had to repeat the bluff before moving forward to a junction at Km119, where a road led north parallel to the canal. As it was now 1600 I made a decision to park 100 vehicles and take 20 vehicles with me towards OP Kilo. At 1630 I reached a point three kilometres west of Kilo where a road which was covered in sand led directly to the former OP. The Israeli LO accompanying me declined to cross this section of road in case it was mined. As darkness was approaching I selected 5 vehicles to accompany me. I drove across the sand-covered section and when I arrived at the clear road on the other side, I signalled the 5 vehicles to follow me and we reached the now Israeli-occupied former OP five minutes later.

Kilo had been badly damaged in the recent conflict. The Israeli commander treated me with incredulity when I told him what I proposed to do; he thought my intention to stand on a roof and shout across the canal to the Egyptian soldiers on the east bank was insane. Using my few words of Arabic and waving a UN flag I eventually got the attention of an Egyptian officer, who I could see was a Major. I asked him to cross the canal to receive the supplies which I had brought. I assured him of his safety. He disappeared behind the sand wall and after a few minutes I heard a vehicle engine start and a Russian amphibious APC appeared through a gap in the sand wall, entered the canal and drove across the two hundred meters to Kilo.

The officer to whom I had spoken emerged from the APC and I noticed he had removed his rank markings. I greeted him formally but he was more interested in the group of unshaven Israeli soldiers beside me. I was concerned that darkness would fall and we agreed to fill the APC with one lorry-load of water containers. The Major had brought soldiers with him and they loaded the APC with the containers, and I watched as the APC returned across the canal. I left the area quickly with the five vehicles and during my return to the twenty other vehicles, I sent a radio message to UNEF HQ advising that one load of supplies had been delivered to the 3rd Army and that the rest would follow the next day. UNEF had shown that it could affect the resupply to the 3rd Army. The USSR was not required for this task and the USA could cancel its nuclear alert.

When we rejoined the twenty vehicles, the officer in charge sheepishly informed me that while I was at Kilo, an Israeli tank Battalion had passed creating a small sand storm after which, it was discovered that they had towed away one lorry of supplies. While I expressed annoyance I was secretly amused at this act of creative banditry. I returned to Km 119 with the vehicles and rejoined the main convoy. I briefed the convoy commander and gave him a marked map of the route to Kilo.

Shortly after I left Km119 for Cairo, darkness fell and the firing of illumination shells by both sides commenced. Sporadic heavy machine gun fire using tracers could also be seen and heard as both sides fired on fixed lines to prevent infiltration. As I travelled through the Israeli lines, into no man's land and then through Egyptian lines, I was exhausted and fearful. I met my Egyptian officer friend at his checkpoint and told him that the resupply had started. I continued cautiously on my journey. My fear of deserters or stragglers became real when two soldiers armed with Gustavs appeared out of the dark and dragged me from my vehicle. Despite telling them I was UN and their friend, my watch and wallet were taken. They took me at gunpoint ten meters into the desert where their military gear was lying. By now I was seriously worried for my safety and mentioning General Gamasy's name had no effect. I realised my life was in danger and with great difficulty I eventually persuaded them to let me go. I recovered my personal belongings, went back to my vehicle and returned to UNEF HQ. I met with Colonel Hogan and other UNEF senior military and civilian staff members and briefed them in detail on all that had happened except the last incident. I finally got home and into bed at 0100 on Monday 29th October after one hundred and seventeen hours without sleep in what was the most eventful period of my life.

I represented the UN at four subsequent meetings held at Km109 up to 10th November. All the meetings remained secret, they were never made public to the Egyptian people and no media was present at them. Following the 11th November agreement involving Egypt, Israel and the UN, talks chaired by General Siilasvuo commenced at Km101. The UN delegation included Dr James Jonah from UN HQ New York, Dr Remy Gorge, Political Advisor to UNEF, and myself. The world media were present to cover the opening of these meetings but were excluded from the discussions. The main purpose of the meetings was a) to reach agreement on the separation of the two armies and the interposing of UNEF; b) exchange of POWs; c) supplies for the 3rd Army and Suez city. While good progress was made regarding the exchange of POWs and the resupply of the 3rd Army and Suez city, no progress was made on the separation of forces. The meetings ended at the end of November, after which the number of daily shooting and shelling incidents increased, posing serious danger to UNEF troops in the area.

Dr Kissinger, the USA Secretary of State, commenced a series of shuttle meetings with the warring factions and with the Soviet Union resulting in the announcement of a peace conference to be co-chaired by the USA and the USSR to commence in Geneva on 21st December. The conference convened but Syria did not attend. It was agreed that a working group consisting of Egypt, Israel and the UN would be established, would meet in Geneva and would be chaired by the UN.

On 23rd December, General Siilasvuo was informed in a cable from the UN Secretary General Mr Kurt Waldheim, that he would chair the working group and he should leave for Geneva immediately. It also recommended that I should accompany him and that he would return to his role as Force Commander as soon as possible, but that I would remain in Geneva. After all that had happened to me over the previous two months I was dumbfounded when Colonel Hogan showed me the cable. On Christmas Eve we departed Cairo for Geneva and a whole new adventure in the Palais des Nations. If and when my book Green Cap and Blue Beret (An Irish Soldiers Service at Home and Overseas) is published, you can read all about it and what followed over the following two years.

DSM with Distinction: Commandant Joseph Fallon

On the 12th June 1979 Joe Fallon was awarded the Distinguished Service Medal (DSM) or Bonn Seirbhise Dearscna (BSD) by the Minister for Defence Mr Robert Molloy TD.

The citation reads:

For Distinguished Service with the United Nations Truce Supervisory Organisation in Palestine (UNTSO) and with the United Nations Emergency Force (UNEF) during the period April 1973 to December 1975. As an observer with UNTSO and subsequently as Force Commander's Personal Assistant and Military Assistant to Chief Coordinator of UN Peacekeeping Missions in the Middle East, Commandant (then Captain) Fallon displayed dedication, initiative, leadership and resourcefulness well above the ordinary. Overall his contribution to UN peacekeeping in the Middle East was outstanding.

Life After Soldiering

Joe Fallon

Following his retirement from the Defence Forces in May 1989, Joe Fallon was employed by the Daughters of Charity Service for Persons with Intellectual Disability in Ireland, as its first lay CEO. The organisation had 800 staff and approximately 2000 adults and children in residential and day services in Dublin and Limerick. The major challenges facing the new CEO were gross underfunding from the Department of Health and many outdated facilities. One major residential building in Dublin was deemed to be a fire hazard and had to be evacuated and 300 residents rehoused on a temporary and permanent basis. An executive staff was employed which included a former Defence Forces engineer, Peter Conran. Within five years, major progress was achieved as funding for additional staff was secured and a range of new residential and development facilities were provided both on and off traditional campuses. EU funding was also secured for the training of adults with intellectual disability in various skills and crafts. Flowing from this, workshops were purchased in new industrial estates in Dublin and Limerick. A number of other Army officers joined the organisation during the '90s to include Walter Freyne, Martin Quilty and John Callaghan. In 2000, Walter Freyne succeeded Joe as CEO.

In addition to his day job, Joe was encouraged by the Provincial Sr Bernadette McMahon DC (a supreme leader) to assist a small team of volunteers about to embark on the development of palliative care services for the north side of the City of Dublin and County. He was appointed a Trustee, Director and Company Secretary of St Francis Hospice established under the Charities Act and he retained these roles until 2012. The first Chairperson, Ms Justice Mella Carroll, remained until her untimely death in 2006 and was replaced by Mr Justice Peter

Kelly. This local voluntary hospice effort led to state-of-the-art palliative care services now known as St Francis Hospice in Raheny and Blanchardstown. The funding for the capital development of these two hospices (circa €45 million) was raised within the community they serve. All projects were brought in on time and on or under budget.

Joe was appointed by the Minister for Health as a member of the National Rehabilitation Board (NRB) in 1998 and represented the intellectual disability sector. He remained a member and chaired the finance committee until the NRB was dissolved in 2000.

In 2000, he was appointed by the Minister for Health to the newly-formed Eastern Regional Health Authority (ERHA) and to one its three supporting boards. The ERHA was established to replace the old Eastern Health Board. It had 55 members of whom 35 were TDs or County or City councillors. He resigned in 2003 as he considered that a fifty-five member Authority overseeing a €3 billion annual budget was unworkable for administrative and political reasons. Three years later, the Health Board system to include the ERHA was abandoned and replaced by the Health Service Executive.

Following his retirement as CEO in 2000, Joe was appointed to the Board of the Daughters of Charity Service. He also served on the Board of Moore Abbey Intellectual Disability Service from 2000 to 2006. In addition, he served as Chairman of the Board of St Anne's Intellectual Disability Service, Roscrea, from 2003 until the service was taken over by the Daughters of Charity in 2008. These three services were also members of the Federation of Voluntary Bodies providing intellectual disability services and Joe was actively involved in its activities.

At the request of a former military colleague, Bishop Ray Field, Joe became a member of the Catholic Healthcare Commission in 2004 and subsequently chaired the Commission for a number of years. He was a staunch supporter of the National Association of Healthcare Chaplains and their important work. He brought to the Commission the principles of integrity, loyalty and devotion to duty.

In 1999 a group of retired officers established the Cadet School Association to support Cadets in training with equipment that the State is not in a position to provide. Funding is raised from retired and serving officers. Joe was a founding Trustee and Chaired the Association for a number of years. He remains a Trustee.

Joe has also been involved with the Michael Collins Memorial Foundation as a Trustee since 2001. The objectives of the foundation are to promote the educational, cultural and artistic training of Irish men and women from any part of the island; also, to promote the training and development of young Irish people for participation in the political, economic, and public affairs of Ireland.

Pro Ecclesia et Pontifice Papal Award, 2012

On 28th May 2012, Cardinal Sean Brady conferred the Papal Award of Pro Ecclesia et Pontifice on Joe Fallon in recognition of his service to the Catholic Healthcare Commission and his contribution to healthcare services in Ireland in the area of intellectual disability and the development of palliative care.

Pro-Ecclesia et Pontifice Papal Award: Joseph Fallon

Soldier, Ornithologist, Raconteur
Mick Hartnett (1941–2015)

By Claire Hartnett

Let me start by saying I would not be qualified to recount army stories on behalf of my late husband, Mick Hartnett. I will however recount a couple of incidents that involved Mick and me, one in the early days of our relationship and the second on the day he was buried.

Within a few weeks of meeting Mick — he was in Sarsfield Barracks at the time, for a few weeks — I arranged with a friend of mine to collect Mick in the barracks one afternoon. My friend was also a nursing colleague and had the use of her father's car. We arrived at the barracks entrance, were verified as 'bona fide' and were given instructions on where to go. We drove the short distance to a large deserted square surrounded by buildings. We upped the speed and started figures of eight, beeping the horn as we drove around. As if out of the air Mick appeared, waving both arms frantically. We realised it was not a wave of delight to see us but frenzy, so we quickly stopped our rallying. Mick explained the 'sacrosanct' rules of the square in daylight.

The following day Mick was explaining the event to a senior officer, I think a colonel, about our ignorance of the rules applying to the square and probably apologising for us in a way, and the colonel's response was, "Mick, I wish some woman had done that for me in my young days." Reprimand averted.

I've heard it said that there is always a funny story and a reason to laugh at a funeral. This incident certainly gave me reason to laugh on the day Mick was buried.

Two of my former nurse training colleagues attended the funeral and were seated in front of some former colleagues of Mick. During the Mass one of the guys said to the other, "He was a great man for the birds, he would travel anywhere for a bird all his life." After the mass one of these friends said to the other, "I never knew that Mick was such a womaniser," to which the other said, "Are you stupid, his hobby was feathered birds!" I could understand this as I was also sceptical of this hobby when I met Mick. That's another story for another time.

The Very Irreverent Mick Hartnett.
Admonishment, then forgiveness!

Adventures with Mick Hartnett

By Paddy Walshe

Mick Hartnett and I were posted to the First Regiment Artillery in Ballincollig in July 1962. Life was tough in Ballincollig. As one gnarled old Infantry Officer commented *"It is an uphill battle all the way even to get yourself fed"*. We discovered that the untrained chef in the Officer's Mess had been using DDT as baking powder. But the Barracks location gave easy access to all great areas of West Cork which provided a welcome escape from the quaint attitudes of the older officers in the Regiment.

Sgt Lawton in Ballincollig Barracks kept ferrets and a young polecat (*Mustela putorius*) he had imported from England. He asked Mick to take the polecat because he became afraid it would kill his ferrets. He was called Polycarp. He lived in our shared bedroom in the Officers' Mess. As the creature grew older, he accepted us as his family but everyone else was liable to be attacked. He had to be restrained under a butter box so that the orderly could tidy our room. If he latched on to a finger it was nearly impossible to dislodge him. A visiting officer was bitten through an earlobe and after eventually dislodging him both the polecat and the officer were covered in blood.

We had many adventures with him all over West Cork. As we drove in Mick's Hillman Imp the polecat would get so excited, jumping between us and licking our ears. Going into pubs, Mick would bring the polecat curled around his waist inside his shirt. As soon as his pint was ready, Mick would open the lower button on his shirt and the polecat would stick out his head and lick the top off Mick's pint. Afterwards the polecat would be happy to curl back around inside Mick's shirt.

One Saturday evening we stopped for a few pints in a pub near Ballineen in West Cork. A busload of ICA ladies arrived into the pub for refreshments after their day out. When one of the old ladies saw the polecat with his red eyes sticking his head out from inside Mick's shirt, she screamed in terror and general panic set in amongst the whole group. Tables and chairs were knocked over as they ran for their bus. The owner told us never to darken the door of his pub again.

The polecat was an established figure in the Barracks for several years.

In September 1964, we were accepted as the first Irish citizens to help man the British Trust of Ornithology Observatory on Cape Clear Island as wardens for two weeks. This in itself was a great adventure. We used specialised camera gear to photograph some of the rare birds that passed by or landed on the island: in particular a Greenish Warbler which was the first record of that species in Western Europe and it remains as the only record of that species in Ireland until this day.

One never had to ask Mick what the next adventure was as it would have already started.

Defence Exercise Graiguenamanagh

By Paddy Walshe

In mid-1967 Mick and I were sent on a Standard Artillery Officers' Course in Magee Barracks. The Infantry part of the course was supervised by Eamon Quigley from the Military College. At the end of his section of the course all students were given a task to draw up plans for the defence of the area. That was "Defence Exercise Graiguenamangh". The night before going on that exercise we were directed from Army HQ that we should not travel to the exercise in uniform but rather dress in "rough civilian attire" because at that time there were serious problems with the farmers which included civil disobedience.

"The exercise will be conducted in rough civilian attire to avoid the ire of farmers who have had their machinery seized with the assistance of the army."

Defence Exercise 'Graiguenamanagh'. 9 Std Arty Course May 1967.
Left to right: Lts Paddy Walshe, Mick Hartnett, Liam Gavin, Gerry Swan,
Philip McMenamin, Comdt Eamonn Quigley (Inf Instructor), Lt Shane Grey.
Kneeling: Lts Jim Prendergast, Mick Dunne.

In this photograph, taken during the exercise, three members of the 35th Cadet Class are shown: Lts Jim Prendergast, Mick Hartnett and Paddy Walshe. The attire speaks for itself and that worn by Mick Hartnett is identical to that worn by Mick and Paddy when they were ordered to immediately sail out of the Port at Dijon in the North of Spain as referred in the section "Infiltrado Communista" in Paddy Walshe's treatise.

We were unhindered by otherwise angry farmers as we clambered over fences and across fields for several hours. When the exercise ended, we adjourned to a pub in Bagnalstown for numerous pints of loose porter. The residents of the town were amazed by the weirdly dressed motley crew. Women even brought their children to the door of the pub to have a look at the "exotic multinational visitors."

An Albanian Football Experience

Wally Hayes

It was 17th February 1993 when Northern Ireland was due to play Albania in Group 3 of the World Cup qualifying games in Tirana, Albania. The finals would be held in the US in 1994.

At that time I was stationed in Tirana as operations officer of the EC Monitor Mission in Albania, with observers on the border areas with Montenegro, Kosovo & Macedonia, reporting on activities in Albania and surrounding countries, in a troubled part of the world at that time.

Albania was a very poor country in 1993 having just emerged from an extremist communist regime led by Enver Hoxha from 1944 until his death in 1985. Five years later in 1990, his communist party was overthrown.

Hoxha's 40 year rule was viewed as a dark period in Albanian history that caused widespread misery and triggered a mass exodus after communism collapsed. The country was cut off from the rest of the world. A pervasive secret police clamped down violently on dissent. In 1993, the country was in a poor economic state and was struggling to convert to a democratic capitalist state. There was mass unemployment and poverty. Working wages were about $20 a week for those lucky enough to have a job. Crime was widespread. There were no shops as we know them. Premises, in sometimes shady locations and with no windows or means of advertising, were where essential supplies could be obtained. Conditions were poor. The butcher's shop was located on the local soccer pitch and often, when the weather was fine, the meat was hung from the goalpost crossbars, with flies in abundance. We got our supplies in a refrigerated truck from Bari in Southern Italy, a 130 mile sea journey which our staff did on a weekly basis by ferry from nearby Durres port. Things were so bad that the road from the airport to Tirana, which in better times had been tree lined, was now reduced to being lined with a row of tree stumps as the trees were all cut down by locals for use as firewood in the winter.

Another echo from the communist era was the booking of hotels. Under the communist system all hotel workers were paid a wage which did not vary with the business that the hotel did. The result was that there was no incentive to encourage guests to stay as the pay was the same whether the hotel was full or empty. It was not uncommon for reception to deny that any booking was ever received by them in the hope that a guest would go elsewhere. We found that you would then have to threaten to contact the central office located in Tirana through which all hotel bookings had to be made, to complain. This usually resulted in reception suddenly discovering the booking.

Also bureaucracy was rife in the running of the state controlled hotels. Everything given to guests had to be accounted for on up to six copies of paper. This even applied to food items on the table down to bread and sugar. All empties from drink and minerals consumed would have to be documented and accounted for. So, the smaller the number of guests, the less hassle for the staff. The wages were the same, or less, as deductions were made from staff wages for unaccounted items.

It was to this scenario that the Northern Ireland team arrived to play their World Cup qualifier and inevitably things went wrong.

On arriving at the airport there was a big delay as visas were not in order and payment had to be made to secure same. Players and officials had to wait for a few hours in unseasonably hot weather for February in Albania, whilst this was sorted out. Then the team bus broke down several times en route to Tirana.

Accommodation bookings had not been properly secured resulting in team and officials eventually being accommodated in different locations around Tirana. Some members of the party sustained stomach upsets from what they ate and drank.

Most team members were accommodated in Hotel Tirana, the only multi-story building in Tirana. Electricity supply in Albania was not reliable and would shut down without warning. We learned to save our computer reports regularly to avoid losing work or to wait out if doing anything that required electricity, as power was generally restored after a short while. No one, however, told the visitors of the variability of the electricity supply and on the day of the match three players were coming down in the lift when the lights went out and the lift stopped between floors. The players waited a while and as you might imagine were beginning to think this could be a conspiracy to prevent them from getting to the football ground in time for the match. One of them noticed a trap door on the lift roof and got up to open it. They could see the daylight coming through the lift entrance door of a higher floor. They decided to attempt to reach up and open the door from the roof of the lift and make their way out of the hotel from there. The lift was raised and lowered by means of thick metal cables attached to the roof of the lift. As they were making their way through the lift trap door the electricity came on again and they narrowly escaped being caught up in the cables. Not something to steady the nerves before an important football match.

In the event Northern Ireland won the match 2–1.

There was a reception afterwards for teams and officials to which some EU personnel were invited. I was one. During the evening no less a person than Jack Charlton, the then manager of the Irish Team, who were in the same qualifying group as Northern Ireland and Albania, overheard the Irish accent and came over to talk. He had heard the stories of the various travails that the Northern Ireland team had endured and was also critical of the state of the pitch on which the match was played. As I would be on the ground, he wondered if I might be able to smooth the passage of the Irish team's visit to the same venue later that year in May. We discussed how the group was still quite open. At that stage, it looked like Spain might top the group, the second qualifying place was still available to us but a win against Albania in May would be vital.

About a month later I received a phone call from Sean Sullivan, the then secretary of FAI. He had been briefed by Jack on the difficulties in Albania and how I was located there and would be of assistance. He said that an advance party would be travelling out before the team. I advised that the advance party should bring copies of the main groups' passports so that visas could be sorted out in advance, avoiding long delays at the airport. Irish passports, for those of the party who had one, were preferable, as visa costs were much more reasonable than for UK passports. US dollars were the preferred currency as the local Albanian Lek was not stable enough to be an acceptable means of payment. I had already made enquiries about the availability of rooms in Hotel Tirana for the party and he agreed to confirm the booking. A reliable transport provider (a rare thing at that time in Albania) was also booked. Hotel management had agreed, on the basis that the team were on a special diet, to hand over their kitchen facilities to an Irish chef and cooks. Sean was to arrange cooking staff and food supplies for the trip.

Jack Charlton with Wally Hayes

I had also contacted Eduardo Dervishi, Albanian football secretary, and relayed to him Jack's concerns about the state of the football pitch. He said this was due to the unseasonably dry winter in Albania before the Northern Ireland game in February and said they would resurface and roll the pitch before the game with Ireland.

The match was due to take place on 17th May 1993. A few days before this, the advance party arrived, the necessary payments were made, visas secured and accommodation confirmed with the help of a young local interpreter. Very little English was spoken in Albania, due mainly to a strictly enforced ban on the teaching or speaking of English by the communist regime resulting in very few older residents with any knowledge of English being available. Young people were just beginning to learn English and were very glad of the extra cash to be earned as interpreters.

Sean Sullivan and the members of the advance party were intrigued by the dire economic situation in Albania. As we drove, mostly alone, on the road in from the airport, they commented on the lack of cars and transport of all types and the poor state of the roads. Hotel Tirana, where they stayed, was a step above other hostelries but still had its sometimes amusing problems. They never seemed to boil the water when making tea and so, despite requests to the contrary, it was always lukewarm. Much to their amusement was the discovery that some of the toilet cisterns filled up with boiling water (they should have used it to make the tea). One remarked that he was in danger of being scalded if he delayed getting up. They wanted to have a meal out the evening before the team arrived but there were no restaurants as such. We had discovered premises known as "the French Restaurant" which was sometimes frequented by European people working in Tirana. It was a shabby enough building which didn't look like a restaurant but, with a French chef, the food was good and we had an enjoyable evening there. However, the best meal I had since arriving in Albania was the one with the team in Hotel Tirana on the evening before the match, cooked by the Irish Chef using Irish ingredients.

The soccer stadium in Tirana resembled in some respects a Roman amphitheatre. The pitch was much improved. Eduardo Dervishivi, good to his word, had reseeded, cut, rolled and, helped by growth in a wet spring, produced a much better surface than for the previous game with Northern Ireland. The stands, however, consisted of rows of concrete blocks, some with boards on top for sitting and some without for standing. There was a small stand area at midfield, resembling the emperor's stand at events in ancient Rome, to seat invited guests, of which I was one. We had an excellent view of the match from this VIP stand. The rest of the stadium was filled with mainly Albanian supporters who kept up an intimidating low roar throughout the game which rose or lowered according to how well their team was progressing. The surprising thing was that there were a few hundred Irish supporters in one area who, we concluded, must have made the long journey by road through Greece and over dangerous mountain roads up through southern Albania, to get to Tirana.

The match itself started off badly for the Irish when Albania got the first goal after only 8 mins, leading Sean Sullivan to remark that his job was now on the line. However, Steve Stanton managed to equalise after 12 mins with a well placed free kick. It was heading for a draw when Tony Cascarino scored with a header from a corner on 77 mins. Ireland then held on comfortably enough for a win that ultimately helped qualify them for the World cup finals in the US. A 1–1 draw in Belfast against Northern Ireland the following November, in a very hostile atmosphere, was sufficient to achieve the second qualifying spot.

The FAI was very appreciative of the help afforded to them for their nervy Albanian adventure. I was gifted six premium seat tickets to the round one qualifying match of the World Cup finals the following year against Italy in Giants Stadium in New York, which Ireland famously won 1–0.

A great end to my Albanian football experience.

Blisters after a route march

The Best Year of Your Life

Eddie Heskin

I was selected to attend the US Army Command and General Staff course in 1977. I was deputy governor of The Curragh Military Detention Barracks at that time, dealing with civilian prisoners, under the Military Custody Act of 1972, so the decision to accept was easy. I had some briefings and meetings with others who had completed the course and prepared to move to Leavenworth, Kansas in August of 1977.

CGSC Ft. Leavenworth
Graduate E. Heskin. 1978

The college was very helpful and supportive as they appointed for you a military sponsor and local civilian sponsors in both Leavenworth and Kansas city. Many of you may remember in our cadet camp in Falcarragh in 1962, we had a visit from the US military attache, Col O'Brien, and his son, a West Point cadet. The son Frank, then a major, was my military sponsor for the duration and he and his family were most helpful at all times.

I was accompanied by my family, my wife and three children. We lived off post in the 'city' of Leavenworth, and the children attended local schools.

The course itself was conducted over a full academic year. There were 1009 US officers, the vast majority Army with Air Force, Marines, and Navy. There were also 94 'allied' officers, i.e. non-American.

Most European countries that were not behind the then 'iron curtain' were represented, plus others from South America, Africa, the Middle East, Asia, Canada and Australia. The course was fine and I won't bore you with any details. What I will describe is how the 'allies' — mostly the European element — organised an annual letter, which each participant sent to an appointed coordinator. The coordinator assembled all the letters and sent a full package to each participating member before Christmas each year. It was also agreed that a reunion of the European group would be held every second year, which would be organised by an officer in an agreed country.

The coordinator is still Gen Adi Radeaur, an Austrian who is well known to some Irish officers as he was at one time Force Commander of UNDOF and always had Irish officers as his PSO. The first reunion was held in Saltzburg in1979, the home city of Adi Radeaur and then every two years after that. Madeleine and I have attended many of the events, missing some due to overseas service or a family bereavement. These reunions have provided great opportunities to visit other European countries, having everything arranged and see places one might not normally consider.

Apart from Saltzburg, we have been to Copenhagen twice, Berlin twice, The Hague, Bordeaux, Brussels, Bruges, Stockholm, Stavanger, Vienna, and Nairn/Inverness. I held the Irish re-union in 2001. I was under pressure in Bruges last year to do it again in 2023, but suggested that planning that far at our age was a little presumptuous. I did however say that I would consider it at our next meeting in 2021.

The Hague, Holland. The class photo in national dress, 1985.
Eddie and Madeline are left rear.

Ireland 2001, hosted by President McAleese, Áras an Uachtaráin

Walking Europe in Retirement

2001–2020

Kieran Jordan

My first walk was on the Camino Frances from Roncesvalles to Santiago de Compostela in 2001. The journey lasted a month and covered seven hundred and fifty kilometres. By 2020, the number of walks stood at seventeen and the total distance was almost 10,000 km.

This first walk was the start of a most interesting and fulfilling part of my life. The Camino has been described as a rite of passage into retirement. Letting go of the army and moving into the freedom of civilian life can be a difficult transition. They say there is nothing as ex as an ex officer, and some find the change more difficult than others. The Camino offers space and time to transition to that freedom, to that new stage in life. For some, the thought of freedom is attractive after forty years in uniform. The Camino is a challenge, taking on a hard-physical task.

Reading about the Camino was the first task. *Pilgrims' Footsteps* by Bert Slader sparked my interest. This lovely man walked many times to raise funds for multiple sclerosis. His book was informative and made the way sound attractive. The Confraternity of St James in the UK had a great deal of advice and a range of guidebooks, which really helped. Through them I learned that there are as many ways to Santiago as there are departure points.

In preparation for the walk a requirement was to read as much as possible and to prepare physically. I joined a gym and started walking longer distances. Then came the rucksack and loads, which increased until I could carry 10kgs on a regular basis. By 2001 all preparation was complete, and it was time to put it all to the test. In early May I flew to

Bilbao, took a bus to Pamplona and then to Roncesvalles. My journey had started!

Accommodation that first night was in the monastery and the few pilgrims there attended mass. The following morning with the first stamp in our pilgrim passports, a motley band of pilgrims hit the road. Santiago de Compostela was 750kms and 30 days' walk away.

What is so special about the destination? Santiago is the third most important pilgrim site in Christianity. The urge to make a physical pilgrimage is as old as mankind. Primitive peoples returned to the mountain or the river to honour local gods. Their experiences have been recorded throughout the ages.

The first Christian pilgrimage was to an empty tomb in Jerusalem. It was Constantine the Great and his mother Helena who developed the Pilgrimage Sepulchre in the 4th century. As the church moved through the Roman Empire paths led away from Jerusalem. The martyrdom of Peter and Paul laid a strong basis for pilgrimage to Rome. Rome had also become like a centre of the church. The Middle Ages became the great age of the pilgrimage.

Archbishop Gelmirez of Santiago pushed for the cathedral to be recognised as another great place of pilgrimage. Saint James (1100–1140 AD) became the patron saint of Spain and a source of inspiration in the fight against the Moors. At the battle of Clavijo in 859 AD he appeared on a white horse and slew thousands of the Moors earning himself the name Matamoros, 'The Moorslayer'. Interestingly, Spanish troops sent to Iraq in support of the occupation in 2004 wore the Moorslayer red cross as their symbol. Franco, a native of Galicia, was an avid fan and claimed Santiago appeared to him before the Battle of Brunete on July 25th 1937. This date is the saint's feast day in Spain. When he entered the cathedral to get his indulgence in 1938,

Archbishop Muniz de Pablos prayed for the undefeated caudillo and later gave the fascist salute to the crowd.

So, who was Santiago? James was the brother of John and the son of Zebedee and all three were fishermen. He became one of the twelve apostles. By some accounts he was not very successful and became depressed. The Virgin Mary appeared to him at Zaragoza. She encouraged and instructed him to build a church where she appeared, and that church is now a basilica called Maria del Pillar. It is another Spanish place of pilgrimage second only to Santiago de Compostela.

James went back to Israel and became the first apostle martyr. Tradition says his body was brought by his followers from the port of Jaffa and from there the angels brought him in a stone boat to Padron near Finisterre in Spain. His tomb lay undiscovered until 810AD, when a hermit was guided to it by a vision of a star. Theodemir, Bishop of Iria Flavia, declared the remains to be those of the apostle. Alfonso II King of Asturias in Galicia declared him patron saint of Spain and the start of the Reconquista of Spain was now at hand. There is no historical evidence that James ever preached in Spain.

In 997AD, Al-Mansur the Moor raided and sacked Santiago but did not desecrate the tomb. It took four more centuries for Spain to rid itself of the Moors. Santiago Matamoros became an inspiration and many churches and monasteries had his statue. As the pilgrimage developed, the fortunes of Santiago and the Cathedral went from strength to strength. The pilgrimage became associated with the scallop shell and the staff. Pilgrim routes were good tourism and a money earner for the church. The routes were supported by religious orders.

Pilgrimage flourished until the Reformation and the religious wars that followed in Europe. History has affected Spain right up to the 20th century. In 1982, 1862 certified pilgrims collected in Compostela. In

2000 approximately 10,000 pilgrims collected their cert. By 2018, nearly 320,000 qualified. Almost 90% were on the Camino Frances and most of those had done the last 100km from Sarria. The organisers are now trying to advertise other routes to Santiago. The Portuguese way has shown a major increase, particularly the one hundred kilometres from Tui.

Heading into Galicia

In 2001 there were not that many on the route. It was never a problem getting accommodation, although the numbers increased the closer to Santiago. Some of the route was over old Roman roads. It is worth remembering that the Romans came to Iberia in 200BC. Spain was a Roman province for 500 years. Anyway, after a week on the hills and Roman roads I felt fitter and stronger. Walking alone gave a new perspective to life and people. As a pilgrim, one's needs are simple, a place to sleep and eat and a good guidebook.

Over the years, I discovered people walked the route for different reasons. Some are religious, spiritual, historical, cultural or plain tourism. A few pilgrims have troubled pasts; drugs, alcohol, violence or war. The last few years have seen former soldiers walk the Camino. Some are suffering from PTSD, haunted by what they saw and did in theatres of conflict. Walking the Camino is a form of liberation and regeneration. The Camino is a big physical commitment and mental test. Brad Genereux has written a book called A Soldier to Santiago — Finding Peace on the Warrior Path. Brad served twenty-two years in the US military and fought in Afghanistan. When he left the military, he found life had passed him by and he did not fit in anywhere. He came across an account of the Camino de Santiago and decided to try it. Walking across Spain he began to find an inner peace. He rediscovered his life again and vowed to help other service people. He established a foundation called Veterans on the Camino. It is now attracting veterans of other countries.

Walking the Camino for some is a form of redemption. Brendan McManus, a Jesuit priest, has written a lovely book, Redemption Road: Grieving on the Camino. Badly affected by his brother's suicide, feeling bereft and abandoned, he decided to walk the Camino. When he reached Santiago, his walk took him on to Finisterre — 'the end of the earth'. There he discovered a pilgrim ritual of burning something personal that brings peace and acceptance.

My route through Pamplona, Burgos and Leon did not present any great problems. The weather was mixed, but with the right gear I soldiered on. It was good to get on the road early and I tried to see the sunrise in the morning and finish early. This ensured a good spot in the albergues and a hot shower. It also meant being able to wash and hang out clothes to dry. People ask about fitness needed on the walk. Many of the people I met were not particularly fit. They got stronger as they walked each day. The secret was not to attempt too much in the early stages. Good footwear was essential to prevent blisters.

After Leon the route took about six days to reach O'Cebreiro, the beginning of Galicia. There is a climb up to the village, and I remember it well as I got lost. It was a Sunday, so I got mass and offered it up. That afternoon in a café, it dawned on me that Sir John Moore had come this way in late December 1808, on his way to Coruna. The British army was in disarray being pursued by Marshal Soult. The armies had passed along the Camino, Sahagun and Astorga after Leon. The army had commandeered churches, monasteries and convents. Having no tents, soldiers slept on the ground. There was no firewood, so no cooking. Discipline disintegrates as troops plunder and burn villages. There are scenes of drunkenness among the English, Irish and Scots soldiers. The troops fought each other over alcohol and men drank wine and rum out of their hats. One historian described the army as half naked, half-starved and fever raging. The French cavalry picked off many stragglers. Drunken soldiers fell by the wayside and froze to death. All this happened not too far from where I was sitting eating a bocadillo and drinking café con leche.

Santiago with Emblem of St James — The Scallop

Back on the Camino the trail took me to Triacastela and Sarria to Portomarin, Palas de Rei and Arzúa. Finally, the Camino reached Monte do Gozo just outside Santiago. The following day the last few kilometres were a joy. The Compostela (document that certifies the pilgrim has completed the Camino de Santiago) was obtained from the pilgrim office and then it was time to head to the Cathedral and the Pilgrim Mass. At the mass was the Botafumeiro — incense thurible — that provided the visual thrill. It is a silver incense ball, nearly the height of a man and weighing 80 kgs. It emits a sweet-smelling incense and requires eight men to swing it. Originally it was meant to protect the

Bishop against the odour of the hundreds of unwashed pilgrims. It soars and swoops above from the vertical to the horizontal. After mass we waited to touch the statue of a seated Santiago behind the altar.

As the pilgrims dispersed before making their way home by car, coach, train or air, I thought that in medieval times this was only halfway for the pilgrims who had to make the journey in reverse. That night I celebrated with a few other travellers and wondered if I would come back. Little did I know!

The following day found me on the Rua Nova looking for number 44. This was the site of The Irish College (Colegio Irlandes) which was rented in 1616 by the rector Richard Conway SJ. It was the place of learning and home for Irish students fleeing from religious persecution. It was opposite the church of St Maria Salome, mother of St James and John, wife of Zebedee. The college was one of six in Iberia, the others being in Lisbon, Salamanca, Seville, Madrid and Alcalá de Henares. The Irish College in Santiago was referred to as El Seminario Irlandes, by the Jesuits. Around 1626 students went from Santiago to Salamanca to complete their studies. In 1770 after the expulsion of the Jesuits, the college was taken over by the state. It is a pity that so few Irish Pilgrims are aware of the existence of the Irish college.

The Irish connection to Galicia has been widely documented. The Irish were familiar with Spain and France through the wine trade. Many Irish ports were associated with the trade including Dublin, Drogheda, Youghal, Cork, Dingle and Galway. Dublin pilgrims were familiar with St James' Gate. Spain was happy to exercise influence over the Irish to the annoyance of the English monarchy. Irish pilgrims to Santiago were responsible for the Franciscan order establishing itself in Ireland in 1241.

Doctor Walter Starkie, an Irish scholar, claimed that in the middle ages Spanish knights came to St. Patrick's Purgatory in Ireland. Starkie wrote The Road to Santiago in 1957. He was a former director of the Abbey Theatre and held the chair of Spanish and Italian in Trinity College in 1926. He was a member of the British Council in Madrid and was believed to have worked for MI6. In 1954 he walked to Santiago and as his musical offering to St James he played the ancient lament composed on the death of Eoghan Roe O'Neill in 1649.

In the summer of 2004 four bodies were re-interred in Mullingar cathedral from the medieval Augustinian Priory. Several other skeletons were discovered in the same site, all wearing the scallop shells of the emblems of Santiago. These pilgrims would have travelled from St James' Gate Dublin to Coruna on foot to Santiago. Legend has it that Red Hugh O'Donnell visited Santiago, given its importance as a Christian shrine and a reputed place of miracles. He sailed with the Spanish commander Pedro de Zubicr, accompanied by his chaplain Father Conry. The group are said to have landed at Coruna.

Travelling back to Ireland I never thought I would return as a pilgrim. However, in 2002 on 25th April I was at the cathedral in Seville getting the first stamp on the pilgrim passport for the Via de la Plata.

This was a 1000 km walk that would be of particular interest to me as a member of the Connaught Rangers Association. The first Battalion of the Connaught Rangers saw action at Badajoz-Fuentes de Oñoro and Ciudad Rodrigo. At Salamanca they captured the 'Jingling Johnnie', their famous war trophy, from the French regiment. All these places were close to or on the Via de la Plata. More importantly, the Rangers were the unit my grandfather served in and five of my granduncles. It was an experience going over that route and remembering the Irish who fought on the French and British side during the Peninsular War. The route went due north through Zatra–Merida–Caceres and Salamanca. This city is steeped in history and a joy to visit, situated about halfway on the Via de la Plata. Accommodation was not nearly as plentiful along this route and less well sign posted. It was also on this route I met Manfred Steimuller from Munich. We shared accommodation and he became a walking companion for the next 15 years. After Salamanca we went through Zamora, Verin, Orense and finally into Santiago.

That particular walk was done to raise funds for the Alzheimer Society in Limerick-Clare-Galway. Rusty Keane, a cadet classmate, was their representative in Limerick. At the conclusion of the walk a cheque was presented to the society at a lunch at Renmore barracks. Sitting beside me that day was Dave Taylor, another classmate suffering from Alzheimer's and since passed on, ar dheis lamh dé go raibh a anam dilis.

I was to make several more trips in Spain and Portugal, all enjoyable but on different routes. Walking in Spain and Portugal accounted for nine journeys and a total distance of 6000km. These routes were mostly on the Camino de Santiago. The exception was the Rota Vicentia to Cabo de S Vicente in Portugal. The other route was the GR7 in Malaga and Granada provinces. During this time, I also decided to take up Spanish lessons with a teacher in Limerick so I could engage with the people I met along the way, plus it's always handy to know what you are ordering to eat!

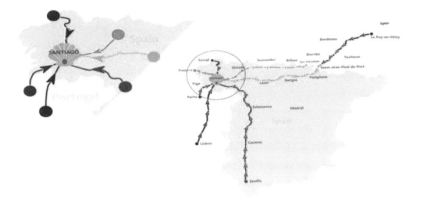

Camino Routes through Spain, Portugal & France

The Traumpfad (dream path) in 2003 from Munich to Venice involved a twenty-eight day walk of almost 500km and involved altitudes in excess of 2500 metres. The route was by way of the Karwendel Alps, Zillertaler Alpen and the Dolomites. Spectacular views and the Dolomites are truly majestic, they are known as the Mountains of Coral. We passed along the lower slopes of the Marmolada, which at 3340 metres was the highest point on the walk. This area figured prominently in World War I and there are now peace walks being developed in this area. Innsbruck was a detour and we spent time there resting. Most of the journey was in the mountains and we stayed in mountain hostels. I had become a member of the Bavarian Alpine club so could avail of all the facilities. The hostels were well appointed and supervised, hot meals were available and most even had a bar! One morning I watched as a helicopter resupplied a hutte in the Zillertaler Alpen, items carried up in a huge net slung from the underside of the helicopter. When we crossed from Austria to Italy, we were in the area of Tyrol, a disputed location given to Italy after WWI. The locals in the cafés spoke German or English but refused to speak Italian. At Belluno the trail came back to the roads and we said goodbye to the Alpen Huttes, we were now

125km from Venice. On arrival in Venice I got a room in a guesthouse on Rue d'Assassin. I was told the best way to see St. Mark's Square was early in the morning, so I was there by 7am and it was almost empty. A group of Japanese tourists had beaten me to it. I had enjoyed the trip and it truly was a dream trek. Before leaving Venice Manfred and I agreed to go back to Spain the following year and walk the northern coastal route to Santiago.

Camino del Norte on the coastal route from Irun to Santiago runs parallel to the Cantabrian sea and was one of the main trails for the pilgrimage. It offered ancient roads free from Moorish domination. One route took in San Sebastian and Bilbao. It also took us through Guernika. This town and nearby Durango were blitzed by the German Luftwaffe in 1937. Death and fire rained from the sky. This was the invention of blanket incendiary bombing of civilian targets. It was the preparation for the bombing of Warsaw, Coventry and London. The famous painting of Guernica by Picasso has been viewed by millions.

Walking through these areas the presence of ETA could be felt. As an Irishman I was considered sympatico and embraced. When I tried to explain that I came as a peregrino (pilgrim) some people just smiled. After Bilbao the way took us in through Laredo and Santona to Santander. A day's walk beyond Santander was Santillana del Mar. This was one of the prettiest villages on the route. The prehistoric caves of Altamira lie 2km west of Santillano. They date from 12,000 BC. They consist of a series of caverns covered in paintings of bulls, bison and other animals etched in red and black. They were discovered in the 1870s in near-perfect condition. This whole route was a very refreshing walk close to the coast. The weather generally stayed good. After Ribadeo we left the coast and headed inland to Mondonedo and Vilalbe. One of the last stops before joining the French way was the monastery of Sobrado. We were invited to dine with the monks that night. From there it was on to Santa Maria de Arzua and on into Santiago. It was a most enjoyable journey although we only met about a dozen pilgrims. We had walked 830kms.

Crete was another interesting route in 2005 on the E4, a distance of 500km called the Epsilon Tessara. The E4 is a longer European route that actually starts in Gibraltar and the Creton section is the last leg. The path runs from Kastelli Kissamos in the west to Kato Zakros on the east coast. The route goes through White Mountains and the Psiloritis range and mountain plain of Lasithi. The highlight of this journey was the 7km walk through the famous Imbros Gorge. Many of the retreating allied troops came through this gorge during the battle for Crete in 1941. We also walked the route of Patrick Leigh Fermor, famous for kidnapping the German general Heinrich Kreipe in 1944 outside Heraklion and bringing him back over the mountains to the Libyan Sea and transporting him back to Alexandria via submarine.

Manfred and I in Santiago

The following year saw me revisit Cyprus walking. It was interesting to come back to a place where I had served overseas in 1965 and again in 1973. The island is still beautiful, and the route is also part of the E4. It had been newly opened by the Cypriot government to encourage walkers and I reckon we were one of the first to enjoy it. Unfortunately, most of the way marking signs had been used by the locals for target practice and so were next to useless.

2007 was the most physically demanding of all the walks I have done. It required high levels of preparation and fitness. The trail on the GR5 from Lake Geneva to Nice is part of a European long-distance route to the E2, which starts at Ostend on Belgium coast. The section I walked was the Grande Traversee des Alpes, which is just over 660km and took about thirty days. The starting point, St Gingolph, was reached by bus/train from Geneva. Accommodation along the way consisted of refuges shelters, gites d'etape and inns. The refuges/hostels were mainly located in the high country and varied in price and standards.

A good guidebook was an essential and mine was a Cicerone guide written by Martin Collins. He first walked the GR5 in 1981 and has written over twenty books for walking. I also had a number of maps for the route. Maps were essential for three reasons: a navigational aid in mist or if the trail was missed; second to allow you to search for an alternative route if weather turned poor; third to allow you identify features from the landscape to get your bearings. The route was well marked. It was also important to have the proper clothing and equipment. The weather changed and tended to get warmer as I walked south. Sometimes the weather variation was dramatic, particularly on the higher paths. Layers and versatility were the key to coping with weather and temperature changes. Spare dry clothing was essential and good for the morale/mood after a damp day walking. A wide brimmed hat and sunglasses to protect the neck and eyes. Boots and socks should be worn-in and comfortable, with good treads to reduce soreness and tiredness. It also gives a better grip walking in snowy areas and on steep slopes.

I started at the beginning of July when the way was free from snow except at the highest slopes. This was probably the latest start for me ever. I also had good insect repellent and a three-season sleeping bag for overnights above 2000 metres. This time I had also packed a good first aid kit in my rucksack.

My previous training stood to me and made the hike more enjoyable. I kept my gear in good condition and ensured the weight of the rucksack was as light as possible. The gradients in the Alps are steep and the ascents and descents longer than anything I had encountered in Ireland. My guidebook had given me all this information beforehand.

The GR5 taught me to plan the walk carefully. My companion Manfred had experience of mountain hiking and climbing and he was a great teacher. Planning helped to avoid exhaustion and we took great care to have the most up to date information on the weather. Something learned was to avoid summits and ridges if a storm was imminent, as lightning travels along them. Another tip I learned was to get rid of my walking poles in a lightning storm.

The route took us south almost in a direct line. The first stage took 6 days to reach Les Houches. We reached Le Brevent without any problems. It was the highest point on the GR5 that we walked at 2525 metres. From there we took a cable car to Chamonix. On the way we could look down to the Chamonix valley over 3500 meters below. The second stage took about five days and took us through the valley. The mountains were of moderate height and we could see across to Mont Blanc. The highest point was Col de Bresson at 2471 metres. Landry was at the end of this stage.

Stage 3 took us to Mondane. Now we were starting to see the local wildlife, marmots, chamois and mountain ibex. In total this stage also took five days. Modane is 1000 metres and has all the facilities required for accommodation. The GR5 was crossing the Hautes-Alpes and the next stage to Ceillac would take about five days. The weather was milder and sunnier. Halfway through this stage was Briancon, the ancient centre of this region. We were now in an area of alpine flowers and forestry. Briancon is the highest city of its size in France, its fortifications and barracks are impressive. It attracts thousands of tourists every year but also meant we needed to be conscious of traffic. It is also the French army headquarters for mountain warfare training. Finally, we reached Ceillac.

The majestic Dolomites in the background

The next stage takes 4 days to reach St Etienne. About five hours after leaving Ceillac we crossed into Col Girardin. It has been described in the guidebooks as exciting, but I can think of a few army terms to describe it more accurately! It was at 2700 metres. Think boulders, zigzags, thin paths above high cliffs and steep declines. Another climb took us up to the Col du Vallonnet at 2530 metres and Col de Mallemort at 2543 metres. After that was the Pas de la Cavelle which was extremely steep. The guidebook says, "Looking back to the Col 1000 feet above, it is hard to imagine how a walking route could have traversed the great grey bastion of jagged rock." I wrote on my guidebook, "Amen to that!"

The remainder of the journey was easy, and the days were sunny and hot. The last stage took us 5 days of relaxed walking in shorts and plenty of places to stop and have a beer. We took the GR52 variant from St. Dalmas. It was recommended as a more attractive route, particularly the Valles des Merveilles. We finished just before Menton and took a bus to Nice.

The guidebook says the GR5 is one of the world's leading long-distance trails. While the distance was 660km linear I think it was a great deal more when you factor in all the ascents and descents. On reflection it was my greatest walking achievement.

2009 was a route from Melk in Austria to Trieste in Italy of 700km. The other routes in Spain included the Camino de Levant, a walk of 630km in 2010, and the Camino Catalan, a trip of 650km in 2011. A complete change of country and scenery was the West Highland Way in Scotland & the Caledonian Canal, a trip of 275km in 2012.

Accommodation in the mountains

The following year, 2013, finds me back in Spain trekking on the Camino Mozarabe in Andalusia for 600km.This was a journey that started in Ubrique and ended a month later in Puebla de Don Fabrique. It brought me by way of Ronda and the El Chorro Gorge in Malaga province, along the southern route of the GR7, Gran Recorrido. We travelled through the Pueblos Blancos of Granada province, overnighting in the hilltop village of Trevelez at 1400 metres. We debated climbing the Mulhacen which at 3481 metres is the highest point on the Iberian Peninsula. It is part of the Sierra Nevada natural park. However, a local restaurant owner advised against it, as the weather forecast was not good. Andalusia is a wonderful area full of friendly people who carry Christian/Moorish/Jewish genes.

In 2006 Tony Kevin set off with a small rucksack and a staff. The 63-year-old former diplomat spent eight-weeks trekking across Spain, following the Camino Mozarabe and the Via de la Plata, two of the many pilgrim trails that crisscross Spain and Portugal and that all lead to a single destination. In his book 'Walking the Camino: A modern pilgrimage to Santiago' he writes of the proud Andalusian people and the Pueblos Blancos, the Jewish and Moorish people who populated the areas. He also talks about the Gypsies and their Flamenco music. This book was a very good read and really summed up the area.

2014 saw me kicking off in a new country, Germany. This time we were walking from Munich to Prague over a distance of 450km, much of it through the beautiful area of Bavaria. The walk took us from one beer capital to another!

The Via Francigena and the Via Flaminia pilgrim trail I did from Bologna to Rome in 2016. This was a delightful journey of 500km, by way of Florence, Luca, Siena, San Gimignano and finally St Peter's square. A true taste of Italy, especially through the Chianti region!

The shortest of all the walks in Spain, at only 360km, was across Majorca and Menorca in 2017, which was enjoyable in terms of relaxation, weather and the standard of accommodation at reasonable prices. Menorca was very interesting; I discovered the Governor General in the Napoleonic era was General Richard Kane, a Northern Ireland Presbyterian, born O'Cathain in Carrickfergus. He went on to fight at the Battle of the Boyne on the side of King William. His impact is still evident today in street names Cami d'En Kane. He is also noted for putting an end to the Spanish Inquisition, improving agricultural methods and introducing the concept of justice for all on the island.

My last hike in 2019 was starting in Portugal south of Lisbon to Cabo Vicente on the Rota Vicentina a distance of 320 kilometres, a combination of the historic route and the fisherman's route.

Before CoVid-19 I was planning a return to Portugal, picking up the Camino Portugesa coastal route outside Porto and finishing again back in Santiago. I have been fortunate that good health gave me the opportunity to do what I did. It has been the most fulfilling time of my life. The circumference of the earth is 40,000km and I have walked a quarter of it. I must express my gratitude to Nora my wife, who supported and encouraged me in all my endeavours including endless repacking of my rucksack. The last few trips have seen me adjust the timetable on occasion so as not to walk every day and allow me to take in sites and scenery, and to visit towns and villages not on the route.

Hopefully, I'll get to pick up where I left off in 2021…!

'Orders is Orders!'

Rusty Keane

A few weeks ago I received a call from Des Travers asking me to write an article for a yearbook for the 60th anniversary of the commissioning of the 35th Cadet Class. I must say I was reluctant to comply at that time as I didn't think I would have anything interesting to write about, so I put it on the back burner for a few weeks.

Last week Brig Gen (retd) J T Martin, our Cadet Captain, requested that I respond as most of the Class had contributed. So as they say in Cork, "orders is orders". I thought carefully and considered what I would write about as I am not an accomplished writer and I am reluctant to write about myself.

After much research I found an article which was written in 2007 by Leonard Fitzgerald for a book titled Glimpses of Cappawhite. One of the articles in this book was titled Rusty Keane — Reliving The Dream.

**Rusty Keane
Played on Munster
Interprovincial Senior Team
1965 to 1970.**

So I decided to forward this as my contribution to the yearbook if acceptable. The full article is a bit long winded with coverage of all the Matches played in the lead up to the final, so I decided to omit these from the draft.

THE ALZHEIMER SOCIETY *of* IRELAND

Established Respite Care Home,
Killaloe, Co. Clare, 2007.
Rusty Keane

Rusty Keane: Reliving the Dream

[Excerpt from Glimpses of Cappawhite, 2007, by kind permission of the author]

Leonard Fitzgerald

On the first day of November 1987, approximately thirty years ago, Cappawhite Senior Hurlers achieved the unthinkable, by bringing home to Cappa for the first time in their history the Tipperary County Hurling Championship Trophy. I interviewed Rusty in a quiet corner of Morrison's Pub on the outskirts of Limerick City on his part as coach to that team. Rusty still recalls that momentous occasion and the pathway to victory. The following is an edited account of his recollections of these happy days with Cappawhite Hurlers.

The legendary Theo English had coached the team for the previous five years. However in early 1987 he was appointed a selector for the Tipperary County team. Consequently he tendered his resignation as coach to the Cappa Senior Hurling Team. Comdt. Mick Creegan was subsequently approached and accepted the position of coach to the team.

Shortly afterwards Mick was selected for overseas duty with UNTSO in The Middle East and would not be available. Rusty, a colleague, was asked by Mick to take over in a temporary role until the club hired another more qualified Coach. Happily for Cappa Rusty agreed.

The first night of training Rusty was introduced to the squad by the club selectors Garda Sgt. Gerry Creedon and Liam Tracey. They explained the situation and also that Rusty had no experience as a hurling coach. His sporting background was on the rugby field. He played Senior Rugby for Garryowen for almost two decades and played interprovincial rugby for Munster. He also had lots of experience in coaching, successfully coaching St Munchins College to their first Senior Schools' Cup and captaining Garryowen to victory in the Munster Senior Cup. His experience in the army would also be an important factor. They stressed that while his knowledge of hurling was only fair, he was a qualified physical training instructor and would hand over to his replacement a physically fit squad.

At the first meeting of the management team Rusty stated that it was important to decide on a plan to win the championship. Most campaigns either military or otherwise begin with a master plan; hurling is no different. This was agreed and a plan was devised which included playing challenge games against clubs from different divisions and counties. Gerry would manage the team and both he and Liam would be the principal selectors. As Cappa had never won the county championship our priority was to ensure that the team was mentally and physically attuned to take on any team in Tipperary. They agreed that to win the county championship the team must condition themselves to winning ways. If players could survive in a pressurised atmosphere in training it would pay dividends in the heat of the championship. It was also necessary to create a good relationship between the players, management and the coach. Also between the players themselves. Accordingly it was decided that players would be requested not to criticise each other if they made mistakes on the pitch. Players were also encouraged to voice their opinion on any aspect of our training at team meetings after training.

To get to the championship the team had to win the West Tipperary Championship. They defeated Golden Kilfeacle and Kickhams to reach the West Final. Cappa met Clonoulty Rossmore in the final, in what was one of the most impressive displays of hurling by a Cappa Team, winning by 4–15 to 3–10. Coming home to Cappa with the West Title was a joy to behold. The whole village turned out to welcome the team. Bonfires were lit and the pubs stayed open all night.

Once the West Championship was regained it was time to start training for the County Championship. "I felt it was now time to bring in a more experienced coach." I discussed this with Gerry and Liam. They informed me that they still had nobody at that moment. Gerry requested that I stay on for another while. He felt the management team were performing well and to change it midstream could do more harm than good. Reluctantly I agreed but as I explained that I thought the team were good enough to win the county, a good qualified coach would give them a better chance.

By now the whole village got behind the team. Many of the local supporters attended the training sessions. The ladies' committee ensured that the team was well nourished after each training. Likewise Gerry Creedon organised challenge matches with the best teams in Cork. We performed very well against these top class clubs, considered at the time to be the best in Munster. By the time the County Championship started I was quietly confident that Cappa would give any team a run for their money. We decided to up the tempo of training. From then on all training was competitive and players were put under pressure at every opportunity. The skill level was improved and the mental conditioning was maintained.

En route to the final the team won the quarter and semi final handy enough, backs and forwards performing exceptionally well. The final was scheduled for November the first. Traveling to Semple Stadium on final day, the road between Cappawhite and Thurles was bedecked with blue and white banners and a multitude of slogans wishing the team victory. The supporters would not be found wanting and it gave the lads a great boost.

Once we got to the dressing rooms it was necessary to get the minds focused to the task in hand. We went through our usual warm up routine. The Cappa parish priest appeared out of nowhere and sprinkled holy water on the lads. Now with God on our side we were not going to lose.

The final against Loughmore/Castleiney was a very closely-fought affair. However Cappa took the lead late in the game and some star performances from Cappa players won the day. For the first time in their history, Cappa had defied the odds and the bookies.

As the final whistle sounded I was delighted for the players and the management team, the supporters and the village itself. Lifelong supporters were ecstatic as a sea of white and blue invaded the pitch.

The homecoming was something else. There were bonfires at each approach to the village. Crowds of people thronged the square from all corners of the county. The celebrations lasted well into the morning. I finally got back to Limerick at about six o' clock in the morning, delighted that we had achieved something that will always remain for me a unique and memorable sporting achievement.

Coolmoney, 1961

Gortnahoe Glengoole's Greatest — Larry Kiely

[Extract from Premier Legends,
with kind permission of the author]

Noel Dundon

When hurling men of old,

Mention stars of the blue and gold,

Of cunning players full of wily,

There's always listed Larry Kiely.

With a fearsome deadly ground stroke,

Premier passions he'd invoke,

Lieutenant Colonel, army man,

Puissance winner and Aga Khan.

From Glengoole and Gortnahoe he hailed,

Larry Kiely never failed,

To break down pillars of defence,

Using hurling common sense,

His swing so full of power,

Cometh the man, cometh the hour,

This Premier legend qualified to go,

to the Olympics in Mexico.

**Larry Kiely,
Irish Olympian
Equestrian Team,
1968**

Invariably when talk of the all-conquering Tipperary senior hurling teams of the mid sixties are up for discussion, one name is always thrown into the mix — that of Gortnahoe Glengoole man Larry Kiely.

Not only was Larry one of the key men in the team, operating at centre half forward, he is also the only Tipperary All-Ireland senior hurling medal winner to have represented his country in the Olympics. Perhaps, he is actually the only All-Ireland senior medal winner to have represented his country in the Olympics.

That Larry Kiely got to hurl with Tipperary at all is testimony to his persistence. Having joined the Army Cadets in January 1961, he was informed, upon word of the Tipperary senior hurlers interest in him, that he would have to play with Kildare. He did so in 1962 and while many of his future colleagues in the Tipperary senior hurling team were winning the All-Ireland of that year, Larry was winning the All-Ireland junior title with Kildare — a first ever for the county and a crown which was celebrated with great aplomb.

"We were brought everywhere around the county with the cup and they certainly wined us and dined us well. It was a great experience and I have to say, I enjoyed it and got as much satisfaction out of it as much as anything else I won on the field," Larry said.

Of course by this stage the supremely fit Larry Kiely had captained Tipperary to win an All-Ireland minor hurling medal in 1959. He had been in the minors in 1957, accompanied by his older brother Des, and again in '58. So, by the time the '59 campaign came around, Larry was well and truly established. He had come to the attention of the Tipperary minor selection team thanks to his exploits with Gortnahoe Glengoole and also with Ballyfin College where he learned much about the game of hurling.

"I was fortunate in that the Gortnahoe and Glengoole ends of the parish were coming together as one at the time — for many years they were separate clubs but times were changing and we hurled together which was a big help. Then, I suppose the experience in Ballyfin put a lot of the polish on my hurling and I was called into the minors. It was very special for our club to have had half the forward line on the minor team of '59 in Jim Ryan, Murt Duggan and myself. It was a special experience to have club colleagues in the team and I have very fond memories of that," Larry said.

The '57 All-Ireland victory had been Tipperary's third successive title in a row and it came when they defeated an Eddie Keher-led Kilkenny by 4–7 to 3–7 at Croke Park on September 1st. They had beaten Kerry and Cork en-route to the Munster Final, but the Cork win came only with the introduction of Jimmy Doyle at half time — he was being kept for the senior team who were playing on the same day. Tipp were well behind at half time, but Jimmy appeared, flashed over three points in a short space of time, and set up Larry for a goal which killed off the game. And so, on July 14th in Thurles, Tipp won their sixth Munster minor hurling title in succession and their 16th in total as Limerick fell by 3–8 to 1–4.

The All-Ireland semi-final against Galway was staged in Croke Park and with Jimmy Doyle contributing 3–2 from midfield, Tipp won out by 4–12 to 3–7 to set up that clash with The Cats. And Jimmy was to become the only person to have played in four All-Ireland minor finals, scoring 1–3 of the sides total as the All-Ireland Final was captured.

Having won the Munster Final for six years in succession, the minors bowed out in the first round in '58 against a very good Limerick side which went on to win the All-Ireland title, again at Kilkenny's expense. The game was played in Cork on June 1st and Tipp led in the first half having played with the aid of the breeze. However, Limerick bagged two goals just before half time and went on to improve their advantage to the tune of eleven points in the second half. Tipp fought back and thoughts of a revival materialised, but by the final whistle, Limerick had two goals to spare 6–6 to 4–6. Tipperary's great run in Munster had come to an end.

That was not to be the end of Larry Kiely's involvement with the minors though. He was back again in '59 and this time he was captain of the side. They swamped Kerry by 7–19 to 0–1 in the first round at Killarney, and in the Munster semi-final they beat Cork thanks to the displays of the two Tom Ryans — one from Toomevara and the other from Killenaule. A decisive victory was recorded over Limerick in the Munster Final by 5–8 to 1–4 and Tipp beat Roscommon in the All-Ireland semi-final by a whopping 8–14 to 0–3.

And so, the scene was set for another clash with Kilkenny in the All-Ireland minor hurling final and with three minutes to go, it looked as though Eddie Keher would finally get his hands on that elusive minor All-Ireland medal. But, Tom Ryan of Killenaule, who had been playing a fantastic game for Tipp, belted home a goal from a free and then sent over the winning point from another, despite nursing an elbow injury which required hospital treatment after the game.

"We had a great team in '59 and it was a massive honour to be captain of them. I had one over Eddie Keher from that because he never got the minor All-Ireland. We have remained good friends all these years and it is always great to meet up with him and have a chat about those games," Larry said.

While '62 saw Larry win that famous junior All-Ireland with Kildare, he went on to win a Dublin county senior hurling title with an amalgamation of junior/intermediate teams in 1963 having hurled with the Air Corps team. And, in '64 he was to win a second Dublin county senior hurling title, but this time with Young Irelands, with whom many of the Tipperary players hurled when they were situated in the Capital.

Larry had been sent to the Army Equitation School in '62 after one of the higher ranking officers spotted a talent that he felt could be nurtured. He was right, and even though Larry did not want to attend the Equitation School, he had to stay put and give it his all — how fortunate a move it was for him and he shudders to think where his career in the army, or on the field of play, might have ended up, had he been sent elsewhere.

He was invited to Cashel on the feast of Corpus Christi 1963 for a trial game against Wexford for the Tipperary seniors and made overtures to the officers to allow him to attend and play for Tipp. He was given permission, but on condition that he remained in the Equitation School.

"Somebody, I think probably Captain Cullinane, obviously saw something in me and felt that the showjumping could be nurtured. We had always had horses at home and I would have broken one or two around the farm so I was well used to handling horses. It turned out to be a great career move for me but also a great experience which has given me a lifelong interest in horses to this day," he said.

According to the Irish Army, since the foundation of the Equitation School, riders have been the backbone of Irish show-jumping and event teams. Army riders have represented Ireland at Olympic, World and European Championship level in show-jumping and three day eventing.

Situated in Phoenix Park, the Irish Army Equitation School is located at McKee Barracks. The stable block, built in 1888, comprises red bricked Victorian buildings of significant architectural merit. These red brick stable blocks are still in use as housing for the army's competition horses. Along with modern facilities, the horses can be seen being exercised in the 1000 acres of parkland in the heart of Dublin's capital city. Its retired officers participate fully and effectively in the equestrian industry's structural bodies, helping in a major way to develop the industry and the sport into the future. Larry Kiely, for instance, was a steward of the Turf Club for some twenty five years.

The school's establishment in 1926 came about under extraordinary circumstances. Ireland had just come out of a period of revolution commencing with the 1916 Rising, followed by the War Of Independence from 1919–1921, which again was followed by the Civil War which lasted to the end of 1923.

The new State was seeking to establish itself and there were many teething problems in the country. For instance, soldiers who had been on opposing sides during the Civil War had to put their differences aside and help create a new nation.

Under those circumstances — the founding fathers were a unique combination — Judge William Wylie, a Presbyterian from Coleraine who was educated in Trinity College and graduated with a first-class honours law degree to become the Crown prosecutor at the Military Court Martial Tribunals, which tried the captured rebels after 1916. He was joined by William T Cosgrave who was one of the volunteers who saw action in the 1916 Rising, and was subsequently arrested, court martialled, and sentenced to death. The death sentence was commuted to penal servitude for life and Judge Wylie is credited with having been influential in the commutation of that sentence.

Both of these men had one thing in common, and that was their passion for the Irish horse, and neither of them saw any difficulty in putting their differences to one side, and they co-operated in a most extraordinary adventure; that was the establishment of an Irish Army Equitation School at McKee Barracks — then known as Marlborough Barracks in Dublin.

This ambitious undertaking was first mooted in the autumn of 1925 and was facilitated by the Royal Dublin Society of which Judge Wylie was a prominent council member. The proposal was made to the Government of which William T Cosgrave was President of the Executive Council — that position would now be known as Taoiseach. In the nature of things, the bureaucracy of the Civil Service spent some time looking into the matter, but at the end of the day they were aware of the interest in the project by the president of the Executive Council, William T Cosgrave, so the go-ahead was given in the summer of 1926. A decision was taken that the Equitation School would have a full army team competing at the RDS Horse Show in August three months later.

Just three months to acquire horses, train them, pick riders, train them and compete against international teams from Britain, France and Germany was a tall order. Nonetheless, the Army Equitation School under its Officer Commanding, Major Liam Hoolan, got down to work with steely determination.

One of the first recruits was Captain Jed O'Dwyer and he was joined by Captain Dan Corry from Co Galway and Captain Cyril Harty from Co Limerick. Following that, horses had to be found because the Irish Army at that time did not have cavalry. They had a transport unit, and the horses were used for pulling carts and general transport, so the princely sum of £1,615 was spent on the purchase of potential showjumpers. That was in May 1926. Those first horses were named from heroic ancient Irish names: Finghin, An Craobh Ruadh, Roisin Dubh and Ferdia.

At the end of the 1950s and early 1960s, live television also contributed to a huge upsurge of interest in showjumping. Ned Campion joined the squad in the late 50s and in 1963 Ronnie MacMahon joined the school. The army team continued their successful campaign in European cities, and also North America during the 1960s. A fundamental change took place in 1963 when civilian riders joined the Irish Nations' Cup Team for the first time. In 1963 with a team made up of Diana Connolly-Carew on Barrymore, Tommy Wade on Dundrum, Seamus Hayes on Good Bye and Billy Ringrose on Loch An Easpaig, Ireland again won the coveted Aga Khan Trophy.

During the second half of the 1960s and into the 1970s the team continued its sterling performances both at home and abroad. The riders included the new recruits Ned Campion, Ronnie MacMahon and of course Larry Kiely.

"I was very fortunate in 1963 to have been the first to ride a newly purchased army horse Inis Cara, and because I was the first to ride the horse, I was tasked with looking after the animal. I got to every country in Europe apart from Spain, and travelled to the US, Canada and of course Mexico in 1968 for the Olympics which was a magnificent experience. Here I was rubbing shoulders with elite athletes when we were having our breakfast — Noel Carroll was the most famous of the Irish representatives at the time. But we knew going out that we weren't in with much of a chance. Inis ara, at seven years old, was considered too young to travel and the horse I rode, Ardmore, was too old. But it was a magnificent experience," Larry said.

His successes in showjumping circles were many — he achieved the optimum (7 feet 2 inches) in the Puissance with Raimondo D'Inzeo of Italy and he recalls a three-man Irish Nations Cup winning side also in 1969 when he, as the final rider, had to have a clear round to win the Nations Cup in Ostend. True to form, Larry Kiely came up trumps and he also had famous wins in Rome, Madison Square Garden and Germany to name just a few.

Larry shares first with Raimondo d'Inzeo in the RDS Puissance, 1974
Larry's jump can be seen in the
38/39th second of https://bit.ly/381bcGg

The army way of life had been very good to Larry and from that first day in Ballyfin College when he listened intently to an officer on a recruitment drive speaking to the students about joining the cadets, Larry had been smitten. He had thought about going to UCC to join his brother Des who had won a Cork county senior hurling final and Fitzgibbon Cup with the college on a team which also featured future Tipperary goalkeeper John O'Donoghue, but the promise of the army was too great and Larry made up his mind.

He travelled the world with the army, and served tours of duty in Naqoura Camp in Lebanon where he was the Officer in Command at the UN Headquarters for thirteen months, and also in Croatia for seven months. He was also Officer in Command at McKee Barracks and in Clonmel before he retired ranked as Lieut. Col, aged 57.

"I loved the army. It was a great way of life and of course my two younger brothers Eamon and Tony also followed me into service. My love of showjumping and horses was definitely fostered in the army and I'll always be very grateful for the many experiences I gained," Larry said.

Of course, with tours of duty, showjumping and Olympics going on, not to mention the day-to-day work, hurling was becoming a difficulty for Larry.

He had watched Tipperary win the All-Ireland Finals in 1961 and 1962, against Dublin by a point in the first one and then against Wexford in the second one a year later by 3–10 to 2–11.

Larry was now in the squad in 1963 and the three-in-a-row looked to be on. Tipp had gotten over a Ring and Cashman-less Cork in the semi-final by 4–7 to 1–11, and while the display was anything but impressive, there was no major cause for alarm in the camp led by the management team of Paddy Leahy, Martin Kennedy, PJ Kenny, Phil O'Dwyer and Jim Stapleton. But Waterford, Tipp's opponents in the decider had learned from the previous year's final — they had also beaten Tipp in the league final that year by two points — and they produced a great display to down the champions by 0–11 to 0–8. Tipperary had not conceded a goal, but they hadn't scored one either — well, not one that had been allowed anyway, with a Sean McLoughlin effort near the end not being permitted.

"You couldn't say that we were complacent, because we were not. We had been well warned about how good a team Waterford had. It was just one of those days when things didn't run for us. You get those days in all sports and it is one regret I suppose. We could easily have won five All-Ireland's in a row and gone down in history. It has never been done yet in either hurling or football and it was definitely one which got away on us. It is still a mystery to me how we let it happen but on the other hand, Waterford beat us fair and square on the day," he says.

Of course Tipperary would bounce back with a vengeance and win the next two All-Irelands in '64 and '65, with the team of '64 being widely regarded as one of the finest teams to ever grace the game. Certainly, it was full of hurling legends in all positions and amongst them was Larry Kiely, who says that his job was quite a simple one.

"Nobody ever told me what to do with the ball or how to approach the play. As far as I was concerned, my job was to neutralise the centre back and to keep the ball moving out to the wings and into the full forward line where we had the likes of Jimmy Doyle, Babs Keating, Mackey McKenna, Liam Devaney, Sean McLoughlin, Donie Nealon — all better men than I to get scores. Get the ball to them and let them do the scoring, that was my job.

"There was little or no coaching back then. Paddy Leahy was like a father figure to us. He was a great judge of hurling and probably more importantly, a great judge of character. I rated him very highly and none of us ever questioned him in any shape or form. We looked up to him and he gave us the freedom to make decisions on the field for ourselves. He trusted us and told us to move around if a backman were getting the better of us. He wasn't a dictator — we didn't have to seek permission to move and we trusted him totally as well. He was a tremendous Tipperary man," Larry says.

While the 1964 final would be Larry's first experience of the biggest stage of all, it didn't quite go to plan. He had arranged to meet up with the team at their hotel on the morning of the game and stayed instead in his own quarters in Dublin, where he was based. But, upon rising he felt a nagging pain in his side and the walk to the hotel didn't help to clear it. The pain persisted en route to Croke Park and putting it down to nerves, Larry took to the field, but knew he wasn't right.

"I just couldn't go and at half time I went to Paddy Leahy and asked him to take me off. I told him I wasn't able to move with this pain and I couldn't figure out what was wrong with me. I had been perfect the day before. I ended up in St Brickens Hospital (the army hospital) after the game where I had my appendix removed. I had played half an All-Ireland Final with appendicitis," he says.

There was no such drama in '65 when Tipp beat Wexford by 2–16 to 0–10, but Larry had missed the Munster Final through illness, as did Babs Keating through injury — a decider which saw Tipp defeat Cork by 4–11 to 0–5, with the forwards having a field day despite the loss of two of their biggest men.

Of course Tipperary had toured the US in '64 and '65 and Larry loved the bonds which were forged on these trips, the memories from which remain as if they only happened yesterday.

A great man to recall stories and events, Larry points to selection on the Railway Cup teams as being up there with his career highlight on the field — He marked Dan Quigley of Wexford as Munster defeated Leinster in the Railway Cup Final of '66 by 3–13 to 3–11 — that team also featured Tipperary players John O'Donoghue, John Doyle, Tony Wall, Donie Nealon, John 'Mackey' McKenna, Sean McLoughlin, Kieran Carey and Jimmy Doyle as captain.

Larry didn't play for Tipp in 1966 as Tipp fell to Limerick, having also lost to Kilkenny in the league — Tony Wall was also out of the team as he was on a tour of duty in Cyprus with the army.

But, Larry was back in harness for the '67 season when Kilkenny ended the Premiers interest in the league in Nowlan Park by 5–7 to 2–7 — a game which saw Babs Keating and Pa Dillon getting their marching orders and receiving three month suspensions as a result.

Tipp hammered Waterford in the Munster semi-final with Wall, back in the team again, masterful at centre back en-route to a 2–16 to 3–3 victory — Larry scored 0–4 in that game. Forty thousand spectators watched the Munster Final in Limerick on July 30th when Tipp won out by double scores, 4–12 to 2–6. This was to be Jimmy Smyth's last chance of a Munster medal with Clare, while it was Tipperary's 30th Munster title.

The All-Ireland on September 3rd proved a bridge too far for Tipp though. It was Kilkenny's first victory over Tipp since the 1922 final, and though Tipp led by 2–6 to 1–3 at half time, Kilkenny got on top, took control and ultimately won out by 3–8 to 2–7.

The backbone of that great Tipperary team was almost past its sell-by date and the break-up was commencing.

"John Doyle, Tony Wall, Theo English, Kieran Carey, Devaney — they were all retiring and the team was breaking-up really. For me it was the most natural time to go even though I was only twenty six, which was very young. I suppose, I was only really coming into my prime and could have hurled for much longer with Tipp, but the showjumping and other things were making it very hard. It was rare enough that I actually trained with the panel — only perhaps coming up to the matches — but I was always very fit from the army training and from the showjumping," Larry said.

When it comes to name checking some of the great players he lined out on, Larry has little hesitation in mentioning Seamus Cleere and Pat Henderson of Kilkenny, Willie Rackard of Wexford and Martin Og Morrissey of Waterford. He recalls Rackard shaking hands with him during a game when he scored a point from a very acute angle — "What wonderful sportsmanship from him and it gave me a great boost that a man of his standing would applaud a score of mine and shake hands with me," he says.

Larry returned to see out his final days on the field of play with his native Gortnahoe Glengoole for whom his brothers Des and Seamus were playing. It was lovely for him to link up again with many of his former school pals and team mates and he regards it as being one of the many joys he experienced in a life full of sport and sporting endeavour.

arry Kiely (fourth from left) photographed with the Tipperary team in Gaelic Park, New York, in 1964, with Jimmy Doyle, Donie Nealon, Liam Connolly and John O'Donoghue.

Premier legends

Larry Kiely has been justifiably decorated on both the hurling fields and many show jumping arenas throughout the globe. But, one award which really stands out for him was the Tipperary United Sports Panel Knocknagow Award of 2012. This award was presented for his contribution to both sports, and for Larry Kiely it encapsulated his sporting life perfectly — hurling dovetailing with show jumping, and vice versa.

Today he watches all the games, keeps a very close eye on the show jumping and horse racing and enjoys what he sees. Yes, times are very different and he is hugely impressed with the modern game of hurling, especially the incredible levels of fitness of players. He has been involved in a few racing syndicates too with a notable success with another Inis Cara a few years ago.

A hero to many Tipperary hurling supporters of the mid '60s, Larry Kiely, with that fearsome groundstroke which struck fear into so many centre backs, is rightly regarded as one of Tipperary's finest ever centre half forwards.

A Day Without You
(Thoughts of an UNMO)

George Kirwan

The blazing sun climbs from its desert bed
Night's shadows fade into the glimmering hue
Tired blinking eyes review the new-born day
And I as I awaken think of you.

Still lying there half sleeping half awake
I look into my mind and see your face
A mind refreshed alert searching in vain
To picture you in some far distant place.

Then climbing from my still inviting bed
I pause awhile and turn to God to pray
Dear Lord you know my heart and how I feel
Protect and guide her through this new-born day.

All through the noon-day hours in this strange land
Where pyramids and towers pierce the skies
I see strange wondrous sights then think of you
And sadden when you can't share in these joys.

And then once more this tiring world grows calm
A blood red world, a blushing setting sun
A sun that draws the mind and calms the soul
A sun that aches my heart for my loved one.

So when night's blanket creeps across this land
In final prayer again I see your face
And sleep consoled knowing that I'm closer now
To when we meet again in love's embrace.

George Kirwan, "I'm big into the culture!"

Class's 25th Anniversary 1987

Cadet Dance, 1961. George and John with their beautiful partners

George and Ann's wedding,
McKee Garrison Church, 5th July 1975

A Journey to ARC

George Kirwan

In the early sixties when I was training officer with 'B' Coy, 8 Battalion in Drogheda, I met a group of young ladies with whom I formed bonds of friendship that lasted the test of time. This, despite the fact that through the years that followed, life scattered us to the four winds.

Two of those ladies, Barbara Cosgrave and Margaret Coleman, I mention as, years after we first met, they were to play a key role in the establishment of the charity Aftercare, Research and Counselling (ARC). Margaret was tall, elegant, good looking and a great dresser and this is exactly how I remember her when I bumped into her in Grafton Street, Dublin in early May 1987.

Complimenting her on how well she looked I suddenly realised Margaret did not want to delay which was most unlike her. Challenging her about her hurry she said, "George, I contacted Barbara last week to ask her to have you visit me in hospital next week. I am in trouble." Joking about her 'trouble' and how well she looked, I asked her to enlighten me. I can only tell you, she said, the way it was told to me. As she spoke her eyes filled and then she said, "I have a malignant tumour on my heart, I need the support of friends, please come and see me next week." With that she turned away and disappeared into the crowd leaving me gutted, totally gutted.

The gatherings around Margaret's bed were in fact quite pleasant. On the first occasion Margaret announced, as only she could do, that she was very pleased with her oncologist, Des Carney, "He's very good looking and doesn't do failures." Every week members of the group brought a good bottle of wine, which resulted in a line of empty bottles outside her room that night. Following a visit to Margaret, Michael

O'Toole, a reporter with the Irish Press, wrote a piece in the social columns of the Evening Press congratulating the shop in the Mater Private on the quality of the wines they stocked.

On one of her visits to the hospital Barbara learned from a member of the staff that the Cancer Department of the Mater was looking for funds to purchase a mobile breast cancer screening unit.

Barbara came to me with the information and after a brief discussion we decided we would raise the money. As we set about putting a hit list together of people who could help in various ways, Barbara had a light bulb moment. She contacted the late Monica Barnes and ran the idea past her. After a brief meeting Monica was on board. Here was a woman of influence who knew everyone and anyone and was totally committed. Soon Monica had all the women TDs on board, the ICA and various women's groups. It was agreed the project should be given the title Femscan and it was all systems go.

In March 1988 Femscan was launched in the Mansion House, hosted by the Lord Mayor Carmencita Hederman. Yours truly took care of the press release and dealt with the media. We got extensive coverage including an interview with Barbara on RTE's Drivetime. Monies arrived from individuals and groups all over the country. Thanks to a phone call from my then Chairman Michael Smurfit, Dublin City Council allowed us to use the new Anna Livia monument, more affectionately known as the 'Floozie in the Jacuzzi'. That weekend saw thousands of people in the city for sporting events and all were encouraged to throw money into the fountain or into the collection buckets around it. The public did not disappoint. In just ten months we raised over €100,000. During the following eighteen months that figure almost trebled.

Meanwhile through the year Margaret's sojourns in the Mater Private continued as did the visits by friends, the words of encouragement and the words of hope. But as the year wore on, in spite of her best efforts to keep a brave face, Margaret was deteriorating. She was a constant sad reminder for all of us caught up in the challenge and indeed the excitement of fundraising why we were really doing it.

Towards the end of '88 the Femscan committee agreed that we should hold a 'Thank You' function for all those people who were working so hard at ensuring the success of the fundraising project. The Mater Hospital made the Round Room available and January 7th 1989 was the agreed date. Margaret lost her battle on January 4th. Her funeral took place on January 6th in Dungarvan, Co. Waterford.

At the 'Thank You' reception Des Carney, in conversation with Barbara, was full of praise for the work of Femscan, but said that there was a far greater need in the battle with cancer and that was the provision of a cancer support centre in Dublin. He said that while oncologists and their teams could provide the very best treatment to their patients, there was also the urgent need to provide these people and those near and dear to them professional physical, emotional and psychological support. However, at that time Femscan was still being supported by companies, groups and individuals. Also, people like myself were hurting from Margaret's death and not ready to tackle a new project.

Three years were to pass before Des again met with Barbara to discuss the support centre. In the interim he used every opportunity to speak to people about his dream. Many gave him donations towards the idea so that by the time he met Barbara he had a fund of over €100,000, enough to buy a house. As he pointed out, buying the house was only step one, after that the real work would begin.

Barbara arranged to meet myself and Monica Barnes and we both agreed that with a house secured the project would no longer be an aspiration, but something real and already underway. The experience of

Femscan stood us in good stead and we knew we had a very good network of proven volunteers. Des had identified a number of possible suitable houses in the area of the Mater Private and Barbara took on the task of the purchase. Guided by an architect, Chris Southgate, who volunteered his services, the decision was taken to purchase 65 Eccles Street, opposite the Mater Private. The purchase required the services of a solicitor and Paddy Kelly, who knew our team, stepped forward. Paddy's wife Hillary was one of the outstanding volunteers during the Femscan campaign.

65 was a three storey over basement Georgian wreck with a clear view through the roof from the ground floor. Before anything was done, I got my good friend Michael O'Sullivan to photograph the place so that when it was eventually fully restored, we would be able to show people what it once looked like. Following a brainstorming session the name ARC (Aftercare, Research and Counselling) was agreed.

Now we had a house and a name, all we had to do was spread the word. For the formal launch of ARC on 4th March '94, thanks to Monica Barnes, Dublin Castle was secured as the venue and the services of the then Taoiseach Albert Reynolds to do the necessary.

The event went very smoothly and was very well attended by the media and those special invitees who could either open the right doors or who sat behind them. Just at the end of the formal proceedings, Albert was asked to take an urgent phone call. Returning about ten minutes later he rolled his eyes towards heaven as he walked towards me and said, "You won't be making the front pages tomorrow, that honour is going to Emmet Stagg".

After the excitement of the launch it was back to harsh reality. Straight away it became very clear to our small committee of six that we needed to employ a person to deal with the various companies involved in the house restoration, deal with fundraisers and take phone calls from a wide range of people. Finding the right person was the real worry, until Barbara announced that she would be happy to give up her job and take on the challenge for an agreed salary. Within a month she was seated at a desk complete with phone and desk light in a small rented basement office a few doors from 65. The right person, in the right place, at the right time, even though I thought she was mad at the time. We were off and running.

The restoration, decoration and furnishing of the house took over eighteen months. When completed it was really magnificent. The colours, furnishings and the lighting were all carefully selected to generate a warm, elegant and luxurious atmosphere, a million miles away from what one experienced in a hospital. Mission accomplished. That atmosphere was captured by a lady I mentioned earlier, Hillary Kelly, an interior decorator and wife of Paddy the solicitor on our team. Sadly, a short few years later we lost Hillary to cancer.

When it came to fundraising, I was genuinely surprised at the generosity and willingness of people from all walks of life to help. From the outset people understood the importance of ARC, and time and again it transpired that many of these people had been touched either directly or indirectly by cancer.

One day I received a phone call from a good friend who said he thought ARC was a good idea and that he was going to try and raise a few quid for it. A few months later he gave a cheque for €120,000. Another man who dropped in to see the house while his daughter was receiving treatment in the hospital raised €80,000. There were cake sales, coffee mornings, lunches, flower shows, golf classics and even cycles to Cuba. We are an amazing, well-spirited generous people. This early response to our fundraising appeal not only provided much needed funds, it also boosted the morale of all involved and convinced us that ARC would succeed.

By early '96 Eccles St was ready to open. The original committee was now installed as the board, which was added to to include people with experience in the fields of business, finance, medicine etc. The opening of the house was very much a low profile event as it was important to start slowly and gradually extend the catchment area and the services provided. As there was no similar facility to learn from, we had to learn as we progressed so feedback from GPs, hospitals and the people using the facility was very important in ensuring that the therapies and courses provided were exactly what people needed.

As all services provided are free, overheads have to be kept to a minimum. Board members receive no remuneration and all services are provided by volunteers. These volunteers include highly trained psychotherapists, reflexologists, and acupuncturists, all of whom give hours free to ARC every week. Today there are approximately 40 volunteers in Eccles St and six permanent staff.

In 2000 we were delighted to receive a visit from the then Minister for Health, Micheál Martin, who was sufficiently impressed with the work ARC was doing that his department agreed to give an annual grant to cover the staff costs. This took huge pressure off our shoulders and was a tremendous endorsement of the work ARC was doing. However, as the numbers attending ARC increased, so did the need to fundraise. It was non-stop. In 2011 we decided to employ a person who would work full time at the task. The challenge was to find the right person. I then remembered seeing an ad in the papers sometime earlier looking for a fundraiser for the Hospice Foundation.

I phoned my good friend Joe Fallon who told me the most impressive person they had interviewed was a lady who didn't quite fit the bill for them, but he would strongly recommend her. He agreed to get in touch with her and if interested she would get in touch with me. Mairead Mangan got in touch, turned out to be a godsend and is with us to this day.

The year Mairead joined us, 2011, I was looking at a programme on the Olympics when I got a fundraising idea. The Torch of Hope would see two torches carried along the coast of Dublin Bay, one starting in the south and one in the north and link up in Dublin City. Walkers would raise sponsorship. I put the idea to Mairead and her team and they developed it into a brilliant annual event. To date it has raised almost half a million euro.

By 2006 ARC was working to near full capacity. It had become very well known, had earned a very high reputation and was drawing people from as far afield as Wicklow, Kildare and Meath. It was time to expand. We were now dealing with the new Minister for Health, Mary Harney, who had visited ARC and was very impressed. So, in 2017 we opened a second house at 559 South Circular Road, the purchase of which was funded by the Government. At the end of 2019 a third centre was opened at Lowell House, 23 Herbert Avenue, Dublin 4.

Today ARC offers a range of one-to-one therapies such as counselling, reflexology, acupuncture and metamorphosis, while courses and programmes cover relaxation, visualisation, mindfulness, stress management and yoga. In 2019 ARC delivered over 2,000 counselling sessions and had over 13,000 visits.

Since ARC was launched in 1994, approximately twenty other independent support centres have been opened throughout the country. They all provide the same basic services, and all are run to a very high standard. In Cork they used the name ARC, but elsewhere the centres were given names the local people felt more appropriate.

What I have given above is really an outline of the ARC story, its birth and development. Naturally, it wasn't a smooth journey, there were plenty of bumps along the way and countless board and sub committee meetings. But all the challenges were met, and all the problems solved thanks to the great generosity, kindness and commitment of a great number of people. And let us not forget that it was Margaret Coleman's cancer that resulted in a few of her friends coming together in the Mater Private and in time meeting Dr. Des Carney, a man with a vision and a dream. Again, the right people, in the right place, at the right time.

Thirty years later, the 3rd December 2018, I found myself back in the Mater Private, this time as a patient recovering from a triple bypass. That is when I decided it was time to pass the baton to a new generation and retire from ARC. The work goes on in very capable hands.

Speaking at the launch of ARC, Dublin Castle, 4th March 1994
L to R: Paddy Kelly, Monica Barnes, Barbara Cosgrove, special guest Dr. Karol Sikora, Dr. Des Carney and Taoiseach Albert Reynolds

Soldier, Engineer, Entrepreneur

Eugene Lavelle

I spent my childhood in north-west Mayo, in a house overlooking the Atlantic ocean. My earliest memory is of my mother carrying me out to watch a sea battle during World War II; an allied ship was being attacked by a German plane. I still can see the lights coming from the ship and the plane during the attack. It's ironic to think that in my future life, both the sea and the military would be important elements in my career.

After school I joined the Cadet College, and was fortunate to achieve a place in the Equitation School with great fellow officers and men, including Larry Kiely, my classmate in the Military College. International show jumping featured several military riders at that time; as well as our own Irish Equitation School officers, the Italian Army D'Inzeo brothers, Piero and Raimondo, were world class horsemen. Unfortunately, my riding career came to an abrupt end in 1969 at Wiesbaden Show when my injuries were so serious that no more competitive riding was possible.

After leaving the army I took a completely different path, studying engineering in Bolton Street. I first built a boat and fished in the Irish Sea and the Atlantic Ocean — off Mayo again! However, when invited to become involved with the Irish national research vessel, RV Lough Beltra, I accepted the challenge, left fishing and established an engineering company, Marine Technology Ltd. That vessel was facing serious technical difficulties. We sorted those out, and the ship spent many successful years of research. The 21 metre Lough Beltra was replaced by RV Celtic Voyager in 1997, Ireland's first purpose-built research vessel at 31.4m in length. It was joined in 2003 by RV Celtic Explorer, a larger sister vessel at 66 metres.

Overseeing the build of the two vessels was an incredible experience. The hulls of both ships were constructed in Galati, a port city on the Danube and the Black Sea in Romania. That country was still an extremely poor and dangerous place, so the Dutch yard supplied us with minders at all times. Some of the memories of Romania will never leave me. When we first arrived in Bucharest airport, the woman in charge of our security brought us into the city to see Revolution Square, previously called Palace Square. She told us how she stood in a crowd of probably 100,000 on 21st December 1989 as Ceausescu addressed them from the balcony of the central committee building, and how, minutes into his speech, the crowd began booing and jeering. This quickly led to protests and violence on the part of the authorities when people were shot, clubbed to death and crushed by armoured vehicles. As is well known, he and his wife escaped by helicopter the next day and were executed on Christmas Day. While we all know the horrific story, it was quite an experience to stand there with someone who had been present at that infamous moment in history.

MARINE
TECHNOLOGY
LIMITED
precision engineering
Eugene Lavelle,
Founder and MD

As the hull of each vessel was completed, it was towed from the Black Sea, through the Mediterranean and up the English Channel to Holland for completion. Then followed years of negotiation — often very tense — followed by sea trials in Norway. As I'm sure my fellow classmates know from their experiences on UN missions, it's quite enlightening to learn about the cultural differences when dealing with other nationalities!

The most rewarding part of my career has been my involvement with RV Celtic Explorer, at 66m a larger and considerably more sophisticated ship. The vessel has been a great success. Firstly, she came in on time and on budget, which as we all know is no easy task. Some technical information: she is a multi-purpose vessel, for fishing, acoustic, oceanographic, hydrographic and geological research. She is the most silent vessel in the world. Acoustic silence is of extreme importance for the collection of high quality acoustic data. She has dynamic positioning capability and a retractable drop keel for acoustic transducers and other instrumentation.

RV Celtic Explorer

When Explorer arrived in Ireland in 2003, she sailed into Galway which is her base. The ship can accommodate 35 people, which would include approximately 20 scientists. As there are both wet and dry laboratories, different scientific specialists are catered for. The ship carries a deep water remotely operated vessel (ROV), Holland1, named after Clare man John Philip Holland, who developed the first submarine for the US Navy. It can reach depths of 3,000 metres to photograph or pick up samples from the sea floor.

Some personal reflections; we departed from Norway in 2003 on our voyage to Ireland, and as we left the fjord north of Bergen, the sky was lit up by the most beautiful northern lights. It was the first time I had seen those lights since I was a boy in north Mayo. We sailed south of the Shetland Islands, past the Hebrides and down the coast of Mayo to Galway. That was a voyage — her maiden voyage — which I will never forget.

The international reputation of both vessels is very high. Celtic Voyager has worked successfully for 21 years, working as far south as the Bay of Biscay and out to the Rockall Trough. The Explorer has frequently crossed the Atlantic, working as far as Newfoundland.

Around each Christmas when I go into Galway city to shop or socialise I park at the docks. The two ships will be berthed there for the year-end maintenance checks and the crew's well earned Christmas break. Like many others, I stop to admire the two vessels. I feel privileged to have participated in such a successful marine science enterprise. The ships are the responsibility of and are operated by the Marine Institute, but they belong to us all, the people of Ireland.

Class Reunion in Keadeen Hotel. Eugene with,
front: Joe and George, and rear: John, Pádraig and Mick (RIP)

Recipient of the MMG

Mick Lynch (1942–2008)

By Áine Lynch

Michael Lynch was born in Dublin in 1942, and before enlisting as a cadet was a noted rugby player. His rugby prowess was not hindered by his army career and spanned 30 years, capped for Leinster Schoolboys while at Newbridge College and later playing with various clubs in Dublin and Leinster. He ended by captaining the Monkstown Rugby Team which won the O'Connor Cup in the 1979–80 season.

The son of an army colonel, he had a colourful army career himself, serving in Cyprus, Sinai, Damascus and Beirut, as well as various Irish postings. For a period he cut a large figure as the only Irish officer serving with a body of Nepalese UN soldiers. When the Irish UN army mission to the Sinai Desert was terminated suddenly as a result of the bombing in Dublin in 1974, he was ordered to remain alone in the desert until all of the munitions and equipment could be brought safely home to Dublin. He was equipped by the UN with a truck, and free access to all the ancient markets of the middle east. The combination fostered in him a love for a bargain and for commerce that was to benefit him in his later role at home as a quartermaster.

In 1980 Michael was sent to serve with the UN in Damascus and then Beirut for two years, and was one of the first witnesses of the massacre of 2594 Palestinians in Sabra Shatila refugee camps. Later he was awarded the Military Medal for Gallantry for having entered enemy territory to recover the bodies of four UN observers, including one Irish officer who had driven into a Beirut minefield in 1982.

Also while on UN duty in Lebanon Michael negotiated safe passage through an Israeli checkpoint in war-torn Beirut for truckloads of the Chateau Musar grapes to their winery, enabling the continued production of the world-famous wine.

After Michael retired from the Army as a Commandant in 1998 he purchased and ran the Orwell Lodge Hotel in Rathgar, Dublin as a successful but very busy enterprise for six years, where his army training stood him in good stead. He was a natural host and loved to entertain. On selling the hotel he realised a long held dream and established his own winery in Mendoza in Argentina. With the help of advisers from Australia and New Zealand there, he successfully launched his own Malbec and Chardonnay wines under the brand El Comandante. The brand name was influenced of course by his former army rank and also by some possibly tenuous relationship to the mother of Che Guevara, whose family name of course was Lynch. He spent a busy few years travelling back and forth between Ireland and Argentina and marketed the wine here very successfully.

In all of this Michael still found time for regular trips to his beloved Connemara, where he kept a fishing boat.

Michael became ill shortly after the wine began to be marketed in Ireland and he died in Dublin in 2008.

None of Michael's four children followed him into the army. However, one of his sons subsequently married an army officer, Aine McDonough, who is presently attached to Cathal Brugha Barracks.

Chow line, march to Rinn, 1961

False Dawn

The Western Front — Winter 1917

John Martin

The sergeant came to rouse us in the cold,
empty cheerless hour before the dawn.
Not that we had slept, the Angel of Death had smiled,
and we kept unwitting, watchful vigil with the wretch,
whose dismal date with death, would soon unfold.

A blasted orchard now bereft of bloom.
Washed and shaved in water chilled by Winter's blight,
we formed a line and dressed down by the right.
A wooden chair, sandbagged to add weight.
A red brick wall the backdrop to his doom.

Loaded rifles passed down hand to hand,
bolts shot home to perpetuate the myth.
An artifice to alleviate the guilt.
As if the rank would fail to know the blank,
from the recoil on our shoulders as we stand.

A young boy, slight and blinking, underfed,
flanked by beefy redcaps, he emerged.
Merciful draughts of rum his thoughts submerged.
The biting wind piped out a mournful dirge.
Too soon he'd join the legion of the dead.

The padre, red eyed, stubble on his cheek,

dull words of hope and mercy intermixed.

While straps, white spot and blindfold were affixed.

In weighted chair he waited, dumb and numbed.

The earth shall be the kingdom of the meek.

We stood "At Ease," uneasy and on edge,

and waited for the dreaded utterance.

"Get Ready, Aim, Fire," the order curt.

A ragged volley roared, and then the spurt

of life-blood, honouring the pledge.

"Ground Arms, Right Turn," while we were thus engaged,

the captain fired the final fatal round,

into the writhing body on the ground.

The red brick wall echoed back the sound.

Our frozen faces set against the rage.

For breakfast, ten tin mugs of tainted tea,

well laced with rum to calm our fearful dread.

Another mother's son with shattered head,

just one more dead among the millions dead.

Not sweet, but sour, Pro Patria Mori.

[False Dawn was shortlisted for the Anthony Cronin International Poetry Award, Wexford Literary Festival 2019]

The Ravens

John Martin

Dragen Koston felt the shiver snake its way down his spine. He had been lying motionless in the same position for more than three hours, and the cold from the earth beneath his body had seeped into his bones. Slowly and carefully, one foot at a time, he flexed his toes, encased in the heavy combat boots. Then, exercising the same level of care, he clenched and unclenched the fingers of each hand in turn. He knew that it was vital to maintain his circulation, especially in his fingers. He cautiously peered through the netting of the scrim that covered his face and shoulders and once again surveyed the familiar scene laid out before him.

Directly in front of his position the ground fell steeply to form the side of a deep ravine, at the bottom of which a rushing stream hammered against the rocks and boulders in its path. On the opposite side of the ravine a stepped path curved upwards, past a lone pine, until it disappeared from view behind a row of tall spruce trees. Although he could not see the house located behind the trees, the image of its faded gentility was firmly etched on his memory. As a child, in the days of the old regime, he spent many weekends as a guest at the house. It proved to be an excellent base from which to explore these hills and valleys in the company of his older brother. The then owner of the house and estate had been a senior party member and was the chief official in the government offices in the nearby provincial capital. Dragen's father, a quiet bookish man who worked as an accountant on the staff of the chief official, had readily accepted the frequent invitations to visit the estate with his family.

It was his knowledge of the terrain plus his renowned marksmanship that had made Dragen, despite his deep seated reluctance, the only choice for the mission. The position he had selected was the closest he dared approach the house. He knew only too well that close in security was tight and it would be impossible to slip past the ground sensors and infrared cameras without detection. There was nothing else for it; he had to depend on a single shot from long range to accomplish his task.

The toppling of the old regime had been swift and brutal. The thousands of protestors who streamed out onto the streets of the capital on New Year's Eve had vented their frustration and anger on the symbols of authority. Statues were torn down, the red and black flag of the hated regime was tramped into the mud and government buildings were set on fire. In a vain effort to stem the tide of unrest, the military authorities ordered the presidential guard to open fire on the protestors. Sensing the mood on the streets, the soldiers, instead of following the orders from their superiors, turned their guns on their officers and led the storming of the presidential palace. A hastily convened court had administered summary justice and the inevitable bloody executions were extensive and immediate.

Despite the euphoria on the streets there was to be no happy ending. The overthrow of the dictator and his apparatus had left a vacuum. Competing factions representing different ethnic, ideological and religious interests had struggled and fought among themselves and with remnants of the army to gain power. An interim administration was hastily convened under the auspices of an international peacekeeping initiative, but it lasted no more than a few months before being dissolved in disarray in the chaos which followed the assassination of the provisional president. Minority communities in outlying areas came under attack, and retaliation followed retaliation until a full-scale bloody civil war erupted. After ten months of atrocity and counter-atrocity, the moderate factions on all sides were war-weary and ready for peace. The one obstacle to efforts to end the fighting was the man who was Dragen's target. A man renowned for his cruelty and viciousness, he showed no signs of compromise and as long as he retained power over his faction, the suffering and carnage would continue.

Fifty meters from the line of trees the lone pine tree stuck out at an angle from the stepped path. That would be Dragen's aiming mark. He carefully calculated the distance as five hundred meters. It would take considerable concentration to make a kill at that range but he was confident that he would succeed. He had been revising and confirming his estimation of the range to the lone pine when he detected movement in the area of the line of trees. Two dog-handlers in paramilitary uniforms with their sniffer dogs emerged into view, followed at a short distance by a tight group of five men. The personal bodyguards, bulky in their ill-fitting suits, their eyes shaded by dark glasses, were deployed in a diamond formation surrounding the target. Dragen eased his cheek against the butt of his Dragunov rifle and nestled his eye into the protective cover of the eyepiece of the sight and focused on the lone pine. Despite the cold he felt a bead of perspiration trickle down his face.

All he had to do now was wait until the target moved into his line of vision. Within seconds he had acquired his target. As he centred the cross hairs on the forehead, just below the receding hairline, he noted with surprise that his brother had put on a considerable amount of weight. He took a deep breath and gently closed his finger on the trigger. At that moment he heard the snapping of a twig behind him and felt the unmistakable pressure of a gun muzzle behind his left ear. The single shot which rang out echoed through the ravine and startled the ravens nesting in the line of spruce trees. They rose in a raucous tumult, harshly squawking their annoyance at the disturbance, before, still complaining, they settled back to their former resting-places.

John Martin receiving the Distinguished Allied Graduate Award
on completion of his Infantry Officers Advanced Course in Fort Benning, Ga.

Christmas in Kabul

December 1988

John Martin

The predawn take off from Islamabad meant that by the time we were high over the Khyber Pass, I could wonder once again at the first rays of the rising sun burnishing the snow-capped peaks of the Hindu Kush with a rosy veneer. The DC 9 aircraft, leased for the use of the United Nations Good Offices Mission to Afghanistan and Pakistan, (UNGOMAP), proved to be spectacularly unsuited for the role it was required to fulfil. It arrived in June 1988 fitted out for executive transport, complete with a bathroom with gold plated fittings, a fully stocked galley and two flight attendants, Carla from Columbia and Michelle from France. It was now the 22nd of December and all had changed. The bathroom had been removed to storage, the galley was gutted and, due to fuel shortages at the UN compound in Kabul, every available space in the cabin was filled with fifty-gallon drums of generator fuel. The air was heavy with fumes. As we approached the danger area close to Kabul the only consolation I felt was that the merest spark would transform the DC 9 into a spectacular fireball and those on board would know little about it. It was difficult to forget that in the hills surrounding the airport, bearded Mujahedeen armed with US-supplied Stinger shoulder fired anti-aircraft missiles lurked, waiting for a likely target. The stencilled letters 'UN' on the fuselage did not provide much protection, even if they could be seen and recognised.

The voice on the intercom was that of Pierre, a former fighter pilot with the Swiss Air force, now an employee of the civilian leasing company.

"Gentlemen, brace yourselves for a rapid descent. It will be a rough ride."

Moments later he simultaneously dropped the flaps and undercarriage and put the plane into a steep dive. The engines screamed in protest in the thin air and the vibrations from the stressed wings sent a shudder through the airframe. It was, as Pierre had promised, a white-knuckle ride. I gripped the arm rest with a vice grip and found myself gabbling a handful of prayers from my childhood. The oil drums strained against their webbing restraints and rattled against each other. Just when it seemed that the plane was about to embed itself into the frost covered ground, Pierre, using all his considerable flying skills, pulled the nose up and the wheels bounced on the pitted runway. Puffs of smoke on the outer fringes of the airport perimeter indicated that all visitors could be assured of a warm welcome. Through the aircraft window I could see, overhead, sinister Soviet Hind helicopters, looking like some grotesque giant insects, flying figure-of-eight patterns in an effort to deter the Mujahedeen from firing too close to the arrivals area. Welcome to Kabul!

Kabul's Darulaman Palace was built in the 1920s by King Amanullah Khan, using German architects, as part of his ambitious but futile attempt to effect the modernisation of Afghanistan. As we turned into the long avenue that led to the palace, I noted that the majestic poplars which had formerly flanked the impressive approach road had long disappeared, hacked down for firewood or splintered by gunfire. The lush gardens surrounding the building had been bulldozed into a defensive perimeter. The palace itself, despite the scars of battle obvious on the external stonework and the sandbagged emplacements that disfigured the entrance, still bore the essence of its neoclassical design. A meeting between General Helminen, the Deputy Representative of the UN Secretary General, and the Soviet High Command in Afghanistan had been scheduled for midday. My role was that of note taker; a full report of the meeting would be required by UN Headquarters in New York within twenty-four hours.

A two-man welcoming party met us at the foot of the steps. Colonel Petrov wore the uniform of the Soviet elite Special Forces, the Spetnaz. The other man, the official interpreter, dressed in an ill-fitting civilian navy suit, introduced himself simply as Boris. After the formalities had been exchanged, we were ushered into the building. We passed through the marbled entrance hall, up the ornate staircase and arrived at the meeting room. The highly polished table running the length of the room was laden with silver bowls brimming with sugared almonds, brightly coloured boiled sweets and pistachio nuts. Two rows of bottled mineral water and drinking glasses were dressed off with parade ground precision.

Precisely on the stroke of midday a padded door opened, and amidst a scurry of staff officers and assorted underlings, the personal representative of the Soviet Defence Minister strode into the room. General Valentin Varennikov cut an imposing figure. Tall and broad shouldered, the array of ribbons and decorations on his chest bore testimony to an impressive military career. Hero of the Soviet Union, full Cavalier of the Order of Glory, Varennikov fought in the battle of Stalingrad as a young man, commanded an artillery unit during the fall of Berlin and had been a standard bearer in the post war victory parade in Red Square. I knew that we were in the presence of a man who epitomised Soviet military power. In common with the rest of the Soviet high command, Varennikov had scant regard for UN involvement in Afghanistan, but the fact that the Geneva Accords provided a fig leaf for the Soviet withdrawal demanded, at least, the illusion of cooperation. Compounding the Soviet disdain for UNGOMAP was the fact that the officer leading the UN mission was from Finland. The deep-seated animosity between the military forces of the two countries is rooted in the successes of the Finns during the Winter War of 1936/40 when, infused with indomitable nationalistic spirit, they refused to be bullied by the great Soviet bear.

The meeting was business-like, and the agenda quickly completed. I scribbled feverishly in order to capture the essential aspects of the discussions. At the end of the proceedings, General Helminen, through the interpreter, Boris, offered good wishes of the season to the Soviet delegation. My eyes were on Varennikov's face which remained impassive, but his reply, when translated, was to the effect that while he appreciated the good wishes, he considered them to be somewhat premature, as New Year's Day was still some way off. Like so many other aspects of Russian cultural and religious life, Christmas had been airbrushed from the Soviet scene. With that, Varennikov and his party disappeared through the padded door, leaving Colonel Petrov and Boris to escort us from the building.

As we paused at the bottom of the steps, the two Russians engaged in a hurried whispered conversation. Then Petrov advanced with a smile.

"My colleague and I feel that it is most appropriate for us to wish you a very happy Christmas. We would like you to know that we Russians are not all the same."

In the diplomatic climate in which all words are carefully chosen and are redolent with meaning, I knew that the choice of the term 'colleague', instead of the more usual 'comrade', was revealing in itself.

A flurry of handshakes and salutes, and we exited the grounds of the Darulamen Palace and plunged again into the chaotic Kabul traffic.

That night in the UN compound, I dressed myself for the nightly ordeal. In order to cope with the icy sub-zero temperature, I had recourse to a set of thermal underwear, a fleece tracksuit, two pairs of socks, woollen gloves and a winter sleeping bag. As I lay shivering with the cold and spluttering from the fumes of the smelly but ineffective kerosene heater, vainly trying to find escape into sleep, for some reason my thoughts went to a photograph hanging on the wall of my kitchen. The faded black and white picture depicts an ill-assorted group of twenty-eight children in a North Leitrim schoolyard, huddled around a blackboard which bears the inscription, 'Scoil Naisiunta, Cill Fearga, 1950'. I am to the right of the front row, resplendent in my First Communion suit, leaning into the picture to be sure to be included. Beside me, six-year-old Lilly McGovern hitches her skirt with her two hands, a sure sign that loose knicker elastic is causing slippage problems. Memories of hiding shoes and socks in the base of a hollow tree on the way to school so as to conform with the barefooted norm flooded my mind. In that moment of reverie, I determined that if I ever wrote a memoir, I had a ready made title, From Killargue to Kabul.

Then, as the nightly exchange of rocket and artillery fire opened up, and the sounds of explosions cracked through the steep-sided hills that form an integral part of the city, some far away but others too close for comfort, I mused that if I was lucky I could add the words, 'And Back!'

Some Days are Special

Johnny Murray

In the early summer of 1992 he was Team Leader of a small group of unarmed United Nations International Military observers — UNMOS — located in the small town of Bihać in north western Bosnia. Their task was to report incidents in the area arising from the recent breakup of the former Yugoslavia and the departure of the Yugoslav national army (JNA) from the town. He had been there on the day to witness the Serbian soldiers withdraw from their barracks in Bihać and leave the town. Bihać was then put under a complete electronic blockade by the Serb Forces. Ten days later the Serbian troops started shelling the isolated and surrounded population which was comprised of mainly Muslims but also Croats and Serbs, who were well integrated and had co-existed in relative harmony with their neighbours.

The UN observer team were the only United Nations presence there as part of the initial deployment of UNPROFOR. During the preceding weeks it had been considered at UNPROFOR HQ that the unarmed Bihać team were very exposed and should be withdrawn. The team after consultation and discussion had argued that the presence there of UN personnel was in itself a neutral deterrent and a symbol of peace. It was decided that if the team was withdrawn it could bring no further influence however limited, to bear on the antagonists on the ground. The ECMM (monitors) had been withdrawn from the area in late April and there was no obvious Red Cross presence inside the Bihać pocket, now surrounded by the Serbian forces.

That warm sunny afternoon everything was so quiet in the town, with hardly any movement outside. This was in direct contrast to the night before when shelling and gunfire had kept them awake, alert and fearful. There had been no hits close to them, but they were tasked with recording the events and report on casualties to the UNPROFOR HQ in Sarajevo, as they were the only independent source of information from the beleaguered town.

A taxi with the horn blaring shattered the quiet, and a young girl came running from it shouting "Quick, Quick, UN you must come and help!" His Polish colleague had the engine of their white UN vehicle running as he grabbed his flak jacket and blue beret.

As they raced into and through the town, the Muslim girl directed them and told them in very broken English that the Serb soldiers had taken some people from Sanskí Most, and from farms in the hills, but she said they might release them to the UN.

A crossing into the Serb controlled area was hastily arranged and the Muslim girl remained at the crossing. The two unarmed officers in the UN vehicle were directed up into the hillside. Radio silence was ordered as they drove up the narrow shell pocked road winding up and around the hillside called Grabez. They were now accompanied by heavily armed men in a pickup truck, which swung in front of them. The Irish officer quickly realised that his first mistake was the impulsive nature of his response and he automatically blessed himself and silently prayed that they wouldn't be stranded or held hostage themselves. Nobody but the armed gunmen knew exactly where they were heading. His training reminded him that time spent in reconnaissance is seldom wasted, but this terrain was new to both of them.

They heard the muffled sound even before they saw the group squatting on the ground at a wood clearance. More than a hundred elderly women, men and children had been herded like cattle and looked distraught and fearful, as the two officers were instructed / invited to exit the UN vehicle.

As they alighted they were confronted by heavily armed 'soldiers' in an assortment of uniforms and weaponry. These men had automatic rifles, shotguns, hunting rifles and pistols. They looked dishevelled, unshaven and he thought dangerously tense.

An officer in JNA uniform approached and beckoned them to follow him. The Two blue berets flanked him, keeping close, but slightly behind, as they were joined by some other Bosnian Serb army (BSA) officers. Calmly, though far from it, the Irish officer spoke loudly, to no one in particular and said, "we are here to help you and these people"

His own voice seemed to lessen his fear and bolster his confidence in a situation he had not prepared for. The Serbian commander stopped, turned and said, "you can take them, provided there is no trouble or shooting from down there", gesturing in the direction of the Bosnian Muslim lines. Frightened eyes followed the Blue Berets as the armed soldiers ordered the terrified gathering to get to their feet. With their belongings tied in bundles and old leather bags they were made to move through their captors and file past an upturned wooden box.

They had their pockets turned out and items 'considered dangerous' were taken from them. Personal items were also taken and as they sensed unease, both UN officers moved to the outward side of the box and with smiles and gestures tried to reassure the frightened group that all would be ok. On one occasion an elderly woman stumbled as a knitted bag was pulled from her shoulder. He reached out, held her arm and turned her away from her captor. The Polish officer picked the bag from the ground and (in understated defiance) returned it to the woman. She was moved on without incident. They kept the group moving towards the UN vehicle and through the UN officers who then placed themselves among the prisoners.

Advancement towards the downward route, seemed preferable to arguing about confiscated items.

The Serbs appeared to be increasingly anxious to be rid of the burden of these people whom they had displaced, or 'ethnically cleansed' as it would be referred to afterwards. The cowed and frightened group looked appealingly at the UN officers who used the little Serbo-Croat that they had to smilingly reassure them that they were now safe and all would be OK. All the time requesting that they keep moving forward. Each knew that they shouldn't allow, but couldn't prevent many of the items being confiscated.

These unfortunate people had already lost their homes, their land, their animals and pets, but right then their safety was paramount.

The Serbian officer who seemed in charge gestured to the Irish officer to go with him to the front ranks of the displaced persons. He in turn, instructed his Polish colleague to move the UN vehicle to the rear of the hundred plus group and keep the vehicle lights on full beam.

They set off down the winding hillside and after slowly walking for about 20 minutes, the Serbian commander who had not spoken as they moved, turned and put his two hands in the air as a signal to all to stop. Then turning to the Irish officer in perfect English, chillingly made it clear that all were to keep moving down this track. Slowly, and deliberately he said, "Keep moving quickly and if there is shooting of any kind we will respond and you will not be safe". He turned and with a half salute he and other Serb soldiers who had accompanied the group disappeared back up into the hillside woodlands.

The Irish officer checked to confirm that the UN vehicle was behind the group about 100 meters back and had its lights on. He then gestured to the captive group for silence as some chatting had started and to continue walking behind him. They shuffled along down the narrow hill road.

The searingly hot trickle down his right thigh was not perspiration but made him acutely aware of the danger of gunfire from either side and its disastrous outcome, but he knew he must not convey this anxiety to those following. He was conscious of his colleague behind in the vehicle behind the group and how alone and isolated he must be feeling, but he knew that the Polish officer was a professional who would give all of them the assurance that the UN is now fully in control and all would be OK.

Without incident in the fading light and in eerie silence they reached the relative safety of the lower ground.

Suddenly there was a suppressed groan from the group, born out of fear and relief. People emerged from both sides into the men, women and children and there were emotional hugs and tears as they embraced.

The area was cleared in a matter of minutes, everyone was piled into vans, trucks and pick-ups and taken down into the relative safety of the Una river and Bihać town, but into an uncertain future.

As he reunited with his Polish colleague both noticed a heavily armed presence remained behind who "advised" the UN team to return to their base without delay. Those armed men were not there to show gratitude but perhaps to avenge the forced displacement of their fellow Muslims. The UN team drove to the town in silence each no doubt pondering the "what ifs" of their actions, going wrong.

Later, as they filed their incident report for onward transmission they felt it would be but a footnote in the tragic history of this disintegrating country.

If it had all gone wrong, their families might wonder what their sons were doing, on a desolate hillside, unarmed and out of communication with only their presence, their blue berets and flak jackets, for strength and safety.

It was a thought that wasn't given much consideration on that evening.

Intermittent shelling of the town continued throughout the night and for some time afterwards.

"PAST TIMES", A painting by a local artist signed and presented by the Peace Movement Bihać to Comdt Johnny Murray in gratitude for his efforts on behalf of the UN in Bihac at a time when the inhabitants were cut off by an economic and humanitarian blockade and under constant shelling.

The dedication on the back reads:
"To our dear and sincere friend Mr. Johnny Murray. For a long remembrance and beautiful memory of war-time spent in Bosnia and Herzegovina — Bihać and Bihać Krajina, 20 July 1992, Peace Movement Bihać"

FCA Daze

Time spent in Reconnaissance

Johnny Murray

In the late 1950s during the school summer holidays, a group of Limerick Lads spent two weeks training with the FCA from our base in Fitzgerald camp Fermoy, Co Cork. The group included Rusty Keane and Johnny Murray who would later join the 35th Cadet Class. The purpose of the camp was to instruct us on military tactics and the use of weaponry. Unfortunately, from our point of view we had to endure frequent marching drills to the incessant shouts of "Swing up your arms!" The real object of the exercise for us recruits was to earn two weeks' pay in a camp away from home with our pals.

It was a great experience but we learned very little about soldiering except that "time spent in reconnaissance is seldom wasted". Remember to "mind your pillow" as you were issued with "only the wan" and salute everybody in an army uniform. We were reliably informed by our medic that showering was not necessary. Towelling was "your only man".

The distractions that we gleaned while doing tactics along the Blackwater from the older, wiser, seventeen year olds, were that women's legs came in different shapes, length and thickness. Our only awareness of girls before that was of their faces. This was many years before women were enlisted in the Defence Forces.

For further enlightenment a group of us spent our FCA pay on a camping trip to Salthill. As the wind howled and the rain lashed down, military lessons on tent erecting exited our brains. We were forced to bed down for the week in a disused farm outhouse, sharing the space with livestock and rain. Galway was full of pretty girls in all shapes and sizes. Sadly the novice soldiers had little success and we blamed this on our lack of showering facilities. So, probably, did the discommoded cattle.

The next forty years were spent at real soldiering, at home and overseas. Great comrades, scary situations and some dangerous places. Military seeds must have been sown in Kilworth. Nevertheless, there was great satisfaction in giving a service to less fortunate people and enabling them to live safer lives, thus inspiring a legacy of sorts.

Youth, they say, is wasted on the young. With all this knowledge, I wish we could start again.

Time has passed. Won't happen. Can't happen.
Too late for us, but others will follow in our stead,
Loyally,

John Murray

Perhaps

Johnny Murray

My Daddy, he once was my Hero,
I saw him as big brave and strong
But now that I'm older and smarter
Perhaps I was wrong all along?

He threw one up high as a baby
He carried me about on his back
He swung me around in the garden
Don't all Dads do this for the craic?

He painted my room as I liked it
He bought a blue rug for my bed
He got me the curtains to match it
And nailed a great flag o'er my head.

He took me to all kind of matches
He brought me wherever he went
I was made more important than players
To him I was more like his friend.

He took me to school in the mornings
He picked me up when it was wet
He worried about undone homework
He fretted about punishment I'd get.

Whatever I wanted he'd get me
He'd buy, if I said it was nice
He bought things he imagined I'd fancy
He was never concerned at the price.

To him I was just so important
I was made feel like a princess
He still feels the same way about me
But now it just causes me stress.

He supported my efforts at acting
He watched me as I played at games
He praised my attempts to accomplish
Not critical of making a hames.

As a soldier he left me for long times
As he went off to places afar
But I knew every moment he'd miss me
To him, he was missing a star.

He wrote me from wartorn locations
From places that sounded so quaint,
He'd write me big long newsy letters
And I sent him back pictures I'd paint.

His return was always exciting
All my breath he'd take 'way with his hug
He'd bring boxes of all kinds of presents
And would stretch out their opening, to bug.

I see him right now as imperfect
Not always important and right,
His shadow no longer imposing
I've escaped from the glow of his light.

I thought he knew all of the answers
There was nothing a problem for him
Now he's confused in his memory
I must tell him again and again.

His dress code I see as appalling
His mixture of colours is crass
Was he always like this in the pastimes?
Was I blind to these faults as a lass?

He frets when I'm out in the darkness
He sees all the badness around
He's awake 'till I open the door key
Then pretends he's not hearing a sound.

He asks me, oh, so many questions!
And sometimes the same question twice
He queries the cost of the phone bill
And expects me to pay my own slice!

He dislikes the noise of my music
He expects me to sit in his car
And listen to newscasts and ballads
How boring when we're going far.

Perhaps when I have my own children
I'll expect them to do as I do
Perhaps they'll have genes of their grandad
Yet I know I'll be pleased if they do!

IRISHBATT Parade to UNIFIL, 1986
John with daughters in McKee Barracks

UNFICYP, Kyrenia, 1982

A Lockdown Memory

Johnny Murray

The history of overseas missions in which our Defence Forces were involved has either been long forgotten or is in the process of being consigned to history because members have passed on or are ageing, and few records are retained. This short personal story is my reflection of events that took part over fifty years ago, and but for the reported comment of one man in a very senior position at the United Nations HQ in New York, the outstanding service of many contemporary colleagues, some at great personal cost to themselves and their families, may never have been acknowledged.

"Most times you are just lucky, but perhaps, all the time, someone is watching over you."

He remembers the exact date; 15th April 1970, his 28th birthday.

He was stationed as a United Nations Military Observer (UNMO) on the Eastern (Israeli) side of the Suez canal. Egyptian president Abdul Nasser had nationalised the canal in 1956 and it had been heavily trafficked as a shipping lane along its 127 miles as the link between Europe & Asia. Now it was a de facto war front between Egypt & Israel, and several ships had been stuck in the canal since war broke out in 1967. The hostilities were ongoing since April 1968 but seriously escalated in March 1969, and an ongoing exchange of artillery, missiles, armoured ground forces and air attacks followed. This was part of the reason that UNMOs were positioned on both sides of the canal to monitor & report on a very volatile situation, known as the War of Attrition.

The unarmed UNMOs worked in pairs of different nationalities, mainly from disused buildings and portacabins used as observation posts along the length of the canal, from Port Suez to Port Said. Their mission was to give an impartial and accurate account of breaches of the ceasefire and responses by either side. On the Egyptian side UNMOs reported independently as they experienced the events, through their HQ in Ismailia to the UNHQ. From the Israeli side the UNMOs reported outbreaks as they saw them through their forward base at Qantara to the mission HQ in Government House, Jerusalem. As the situation escalated there was an increased frequency of air attacks, along and across the canal. The Israelis were mainly using F4 Phantom II, Skyhawks and Mirage 111s. The Egyptians were employing 21 MFs MiG fighters, which were allegedly piloted by Soviet personnel.

He was aware that other Irish officers were stationed elsewhere on both sides of the canal, including his former cadet class colleagues George Kerwin, Maurice Sweeney & the late Larry Cooke, but there was no direct communication between the UN positions on either side.

UNMOs would remain stationary in their positions from seven to ten days depending on the intensity of the exchanges between the conflicting forces. Leaving the OP was not an option during outbreaks of hostilities, but there was an underground bunker shelter with communications and lighting, from a generator maintained and operated by the officers. Liaison officers (LOs) — Israeli or Egyptian — could be made available in case of emergency. The bunker contained emergency rations but UNMOs brought enough food with them for their stay. Cooking duties were shared and different national menus were cooked, sampled and exchanged.

Some months earlier the Under Secretary of the United Nations, Ralph Bunch, had visited the Mission area. In his report afterwards to the mission he described the task of the unarmed observers on the Suez canal as the most dangerous job on earth.

The per diem rate was increased from $10 to $12.50. It was very welcome.

He had worked in several OPs on the eastern side since his arrival to the mission area in January and was learning to live with the quiet tension of the location. That afternoon his fellow UNMO, an Argentinian, was the cook for the day and so it was his task to do the washing up outside in the shade from the sunshine. Without warning, he heard and saw the Israelis swoop down from north of his position with Phantom and Skyhawk attack aircraft. The aircraft weapons fired along the Egyptian side for several hundred yards and then as swiftly departed high into the noon day sunshine on the eastern side of the desert, mission accomplished.

This was not the first air attack he had experienced, so his immediate reaction was to dive under the trestle table he was working at and pull it down over him. Although he didn't ponder the quotation that "there are no atheists in the trenches", he remembered his colleague Vincent Savino saying that when you are caught out in a shelling in the desert — especially when your flak jacket and helmet are several yards away — you curse at how big the buttons are on your shirt as you grovel as deep as you can in the sand.

The air attack was over very quickly and in the eerie silence that followed, he heard his colleague calling from the entrance to the bunker, asking if he was ok. He was. Just as he was about to get up and run the twenty yards to the bunker, he heard the anti-aircraft fire from the Egyptian side. Firstly the 'pum pum' of the weapons, but as they lowered the trajectory of their anti-aircraft guns a whistling screeching sound could be heard. This was from large clumps of shrapnel from the munitions as it indiscriminately hurtled down from the sky on the UN compound and out into the desert.

This shooting continued for several minutes but they had been warned that this was an extremely dangerous time to be exposed and unprotected. His flashing thought was to be wounded or killed in such a way on his birthday, would be an inglorious footnote of history. Thankfully there were no casualties at their OP and little damage to their buildings. He had no idea of the effect of the air attack on the Egyptian side. In the following weeks up until the ceasefire that August, three OPs on the Eastern side were destroyed and a Swedish UNMO shot on the canal.

Thankfully the next few days, though relatively tense, were uneventful and quiet in their area as they maintained their twenty-four-hour presence. As per SOP they called in their report as they had experienced events. This included the starting time of an outbreak and the ending time of the exchange, also the aircraft and the weapons they could identify. These reports were transmitted as soon after the events as was practical. Apart from being informative, it was also therapeutic for UNMOs as it helped relieve them from some of the trauma of the events.

As per roster, the UNMOs were relieved three days later after briefing, cleaning and handing over the contents of the OP to the incoming UNMOs. Later that night they got back to Jerusalem and he returned to his home and his new bride. They had married two months earlier at the Church of All Nations in the Garden of Gethsemane on the 17th March — St Patrick's Day. The incident on the canal was not shared with his wife. Happenings on the canal were only discussed and exchanged during briefings in the Area of Operations.

This is my memory of a single event at a particular time and is both personal and subjective. We had good fortune that day. Others, Irish officers included, were less fortunate. For all the Irish UNMOs, this story is about them and their own experiences during prolonged stressful and difficult times. All of them showed outstanding capability and strong spirit, spending long and difficult hours on either side of the canal during this War of Attrition.

Let us not forget any of them.

Before he would return to the Suez Canal he had a week off. Next time he was posted to a different OP and with a different companion.

For now he was in the magical city of Jerusalem and he had more pleasurable distractions to enjoy.

Paráid Aifreann. Dalta O'Mairtín i gCeannais.

Eachtraí sa bhFásach

Pádraig A O'Murchú

Ó am go h-am tagtar ar ócháidí nó gníomhartha atá comh as an gcoitiantacht go bhfanann siad in ár n-aigne linn i bhfad tar éis an chinniúint féin.

Is chur síos pearsanta é seo ar a leithéid de ócháid a thárla idir dhá lá chinniúnach i 1973.

Ar an 25ú Deire Fómhair 1973, fógraíodh sos cogaidh idir fórsaí Iosrael agus na comhghuaillithe Arabach tar éis Cogadh Yom Kippur. Faoin am sin bhí Arm Iosrael treasna an Canál Suez san Éigipt agus ag bagairt Cathair Damascus i Syria san oirthir. Chuaigh na Náisiúin Aontaithe i mbun síochán a chuir i ngíomh sa cheantair.

Mar ábhar tosaigh cuireadh patróil UNTSO amach ar gach taobh chun suíomhanna na h-airm a aimsiú. I KCC bhí beirt oifigeach ar gach patról agus iad feistithe fanacht amach sa bhfásach ar feadh ceithre lá. I dteannta siúd bhí oifigeach cheangail Arm Iosrael agus a fhoireann.

In éineacht le oifigeach Fionlannach rinne mé mo chéad patról sa dúiche siar ó Deversoir i mbarr an 'Great Bitter Lake' agus ag taisteal ó thuaidh ó sin, comhthreomhar leis an bealach uisce an 'Sweet Water Canal' go dtí imeall Cathair Ismailiya. De bharr tionchur an 'Sweet Water Canal' is láthair torthuail, úrghlas, tiubh, cothromach é. Toisc an chumas foraoiseach sa cheantar bhí deachrachtaí móra ann na suíomhanna míleata a bhaint amach agus bhraitheamar ar na h-airm ar leith na h-eagair a theaspáint dúinn, rud a rinne Arm Iosrael ag an bpointe seo — níor lean sé.

Bhí sé dainséarach a bheith thar bráid sa dorchadas agus bhí gá dídean shábháilte a fháil i rith na h-oíche. Sa cás seo bhuaileamar ar aonad Iosraelach a ghlach isteach linn. Ba complacht iompar uisce iad — complacht neamhspleách, neamh gnáthach agus neamhchoitianta. I gciorcal mór a bhí an suíomh, laistigh bhí na tancaerí lena rabhadar feistithe, feithiclí ollmhór de gach déantús, laistig dóibh siúd bhí tealltana, ceann díobh ag feidhmiú mar bialann agus ceann eile á úsáid mar áit codladh do corrdhaoine a bhí ag scagaireacht thar nais dos na h-aonaid troda tar éis téarmaí i n-ospidéal nó saoire. Bhí caighean príosúnach cogadh ann leis, le scata beag Éigiptigh faoi choimeád. Bhí an suíomh uilig timpeallaithe le sreang.

Fir níos aosta ná an gnáthach abea na saighdiúirí agus iad neamhchúiseach mar gheall ar gnáth imeachtaí míleata. Is cosúil nach raibh aon freagarthas ag an aonad as an suíomh a chaomhnú. Ba feithiclí príobháideach a slógadh don cogadh abea na tancaerí, le ainmneacha na gnóthanna as a dtánadar fós ortha agus a úinéirí leo mar tiománaí i roinnt cás. I rith an lae rachaidís thar nais go pointí uisce úr a bhí suite i bhfásach Sinai agus an t-ualach a aistarraingt chuig na h-eagair a bhí i ngleic le Arm na h-Éigipt.

Cé go raibh a dhóthain uisce úr le fáil i limistéir na troda, ní raibh sé sábháilte le n-ól agus bhí bealach uisce 'Sweet Water' plódaithe le bilharzia agus galair eile. Tá cosúlacht ann gur cuireadh an aonad seo le chéile go tapaidh leis an fhadhb a réiteach. Dála an scéal bhí tábhacht ar leith leis an aonad neamhgnáthacht seo.

An lá dár gcionn leanamar leis an patról agus, ag lorg na tol-línte, thánamar ar cheanncheathrú rannán Iúdach mar a bhuaileamar leis an cheannasaí. Bhí eisean an-chabhrach linn agus i ndiaidh lóin lena fhoireann dírigh sé ar oifigeach fóirne na tol-línte sa timpeallacht a theaspaint dúinn.

Ar theacht an tráthnóna bhuaileamar ar aonad neamhgnáthach eile a bhí toilteannach glacha linn don oíche. I measc fothracha, gar don bóthar idir Deversoir agus Ismailiya, bhí cathlán Bedouin i seirbhís le Arm Iosrael. Ba Iúdach an cheannasaí, Lt Col as buanarm Iosrael agus ba Iúdaigh leis na h-oifigí eile agus labhradar uilig Araibis. Saighdiúirí santach, lán aimsire abea na Bedouin, iad gléasta agus armtha cosúil le Arm Iosrael i gcoiteann. Cé go raibh feithicilí armúrtha (M3) leo, i dteannta siúd bhí córas iompar i bhfad níos sinne dá n-úsáid leis, camail, a bhí dá choimead le hais an champa.

Bhí sé soiléir go raibh árd mheas ag an cheannasaí as a shaighdiúirí agus é lán sásta labhairt fúthu. Ba aonad taiscéalaíochta agus lorgaireach sa bhfásach a bhí iontu de gnáth agus níorbh fhéidir linn a aimsiú cén fáth go rabhadar anseo i lár na coimhlinte, lena gcamail. Is féidir a shamhlú áfach, ós rud é go raibh Arm Iosrael in iomlán chaite isteach sa chomhraic faoin am seo, gurbh an chathlán seo i measc na cúltachaí deireannach a bhí le fáil. Pé scéala ar an tráthnóna sin bhíodar lúcháireach tar éis dóibh teacht thar nais ó timpeallacht Cathair Suez, mar a bhí troid fós ar siúl, agus gur bhraitheadar thar nais leo creach ó stórais bia íosreoite Síneach a thit chúcha i rith an lá.

Do réir a cheannasaí, níor aithnigh na Bedouin seo aon rialtas ná údarás sa cheantar seachas Rí Hussein na Iurdáine, ach go raibh tuiscint éagoitianta ann a cheadaigh a sheirbhís le fórsaí Iosrael. Gné ait eile a bhain leis an chathlán seo ná go raibh síbhialtach aonarach ina measc agus é ag feidhmniú mar 'séiplíneach' Mathamadach, fear a roghnaíodh dá ceapachán ag údarás eile seachas na hIosraelaigh. Athnaíodh é mar an té ba thábhachtaí sa chathlán. Fear aosta a bhí ann, nár chaith éide cogaidh, ach gur tugadh ard urraim dó ag chuile dhaoine.

Leis na gaiscí a rinneadar i rith an lae a cheiliúradh, bhí fleadh fhulachta acu an oíche sin. Suí an chathlán uilig mór thimpeall tine ollmhór, oifigí agus cuairteoirí ina measc, ag ithe agus ag scéalaíocht go fada isteach san oíche.

Nuair a d'imíomar an lá dár gcionn bhí an cathlán agus na camail fós ann.

I rith na míosanna go rinne Arm Iosrael aistarraingt ón Éigipt, leis an socrú síochána, níor thánaig éinne i KCC ar ceachtar na h-aonaid sainiúil, suimiúil, neamhgnáthach seo arís.

B'fhéidir gur brionglóid a bhí ann.

Romani-Sinai Thuaidh, 9ú lá Samhain 1973.
I dteannta oifigeach cheangail Arm Iosrael agus a fhoireann at tús patról

10 · THE YOM KIPPUR WAR Turas an Patrol

The Bar-Lev Line

Turas an Patrol

162

The Egyptian bridgeheads and SAM umbrella, 14 October 1973

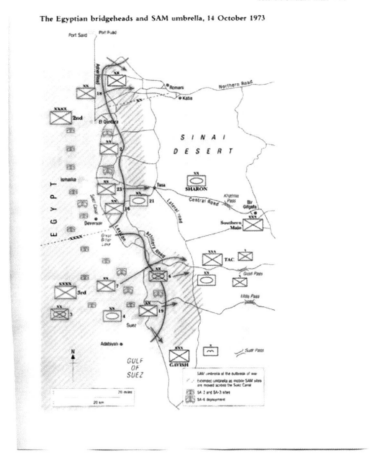

The October War

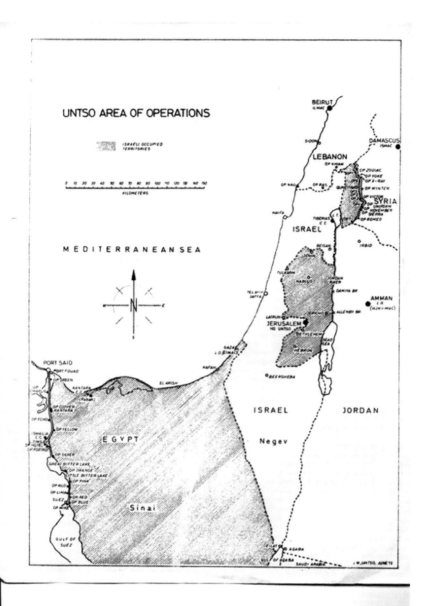

UNTSO area of operations

Nótaí Breise

1. Nuair a thosnaigh Cogadh Yom Kippur bhí ceithre iarbhall an 35ú Rang Daltaí ar seirbhís le UNTSO.

   - Dáithi Ó Táilliúr (KCC) —
     Ar post breathnadóireachta taobh thoir Canál Suez.
   - Seosamh Ó Fallúin (EIMAC) —
     Ar post breathnadóireachta taobh thiar Canál Suez.
   - Mícheál Ó Nualláin (TCC) — Árdán Golan.
   - Pádraig Ó Murchú (KCC) — Ceanncheathrú KCC, Rabah, Sinai.

   Maidir liomsa chaitheas an chéad seachtain den cogadh i Rabah sa Sinai agus an seachtain deireannach ar post breathnadóireachta TCC gar do Kuneitra, Árdán Golan.

2. **An Rannán Iosraelach** Níl fhios againn ciochu rannán a bhí ann ach bhí Ugda 'Kalman' — Rannán cúltacha armúrtha 146 sa timpeallacht ar feadh tamaill, faoi cheannas BG Yitzak Sasson.

3. **Pointí Uisce** Do bheadh aithne ag éinne sa rang a chaith seal le KCC/UNTSO ar na pointí uisce cóngarach don Canál Suez. Thánaig an uisce i bpíopaí ó Iosrael agus trasna fásach Sinai. Sa Chéad Cogadh Domhanda thárla a mhalairt. D'iompraíodh an uisce ar dhroim camail treasna Sinai sa tsli eile, le arm an Ginearál Allenby a chothú agus iad ag troid i gcoinne na Turcaigh. Samhlaítear gur as an bealach uisce 'Sweet Water' a tháinig an t-uisce.

A New Career

Michael O'Sullivan

The Bank of Ireland calendar 1994 was based on my photographs of the Irish landscape. Distributed throughout Ireland, the UK, and some cities in Europe and America, it is the number one entry in my photography CV.

Ground Radar
4 October 1967–2 October 1968

This story began 30 years before. I purchased my first camera — first of 11 — in 1963, an event that one day would lead to a new career. The '60s were the best of times for me. They brought me to Gormanston Air Corps Station, my favourite posting; to Royal Signals, Catterick Camp, Yorkshire; and to a year on a Royal Air Force station in Somerset.

I was serving in the Signal Corps. As the years passed I knew that I would retire early to follow a new career. In 1982, the year of the Falklands war, I was in my 22nd year of service. It was "now or never" time. I retired as Commandant on the last day of August that year, and proceeded to "invent" a new career for myself: I would make photographs of building and civil engineering.

I was single, in my 41st year, and I would receive retired pay monthly from the state.

Wednesday 1st September 1982 marked a new beginning. The government job was history. I was out. It was a day like no other.

I introduced myself and my proposed service to the main players in the construction industry. The first response arrived at the end of October. After a brief interview by a long established building company, I was dispatched to photograph some completed projects. By Christmas, three other companies had arrived. Doors had opened!

It was my particular good fortune that Paddy Walshe, classmate and fellow rebel, retired from artillery about the same time, to set up a very successful photo-processing laboratory nearby. He processed the films, made the prints and introduced me to Linhof, the Rolls Royce of camera makers.

In January 1983 a civil engineering company made contact. They were building 2 bridges near Castlecomer, Co. Kilkenny, and wanted regular progress photographs of the work.

Aasleagh Falls, Co. Mayo. This waterfall featured prominently in the film version of John B. Keane's play The Field.

Remember Castlecomer? An overnight stop in a tented field on the long march to Ring, County Waterford, long ago when we were young. It was at Castlecomer that my new career took off. I visited those two sites nine times that year. That company employed me for the next sixteen years, at approximately monthly intervals, in eighteen different locations in the Republic. It was water/waste water treatment; pipelines (water, sewage, gas); roadworks and bridges; reservoirs, water towers and pumping stations.

George Kirwan sent much work my way. This was in eight racecourses (buildings & facilities) in various commercial/industrial premises, and even included a day trip to London! In 1983, a firm of architects — clients of his — planned an exhibition to celebrate one hundred years of the practice. This required much photography. It was churches and cathedrals, hospitals and convents, schools and colleges, and commercial/industrial premises, most but not all in Leinster. Paddy processed the films, and made the large mounted exhibition prints. Assisted by George, the architects put on their show at the National Concert Hall on 24th November. This was more than an exhibition of fine architecture. It was also a team of three army classmates in action!

What followed from Castlecomer was an adventure. Over the following sixteen years my employers steadily grew in number to include most of the 'household' names in the industry. My work, while mostly in Leinster, brought me to twenty-four counties in the republic. Longford and Leitrim escaped. None were operating in Northern Ireland.

Variety and travel defined my work, which divided into two areas, building and civil engineering. The buildings, which accounted for twenty-five per cent of my work, were mainly educational, medical, and commercial/industrial, with some significant restoration work (Government Buildings and Luttrellstown Castle). Civil engineering was the main event. Every civil works site had a sign at the entrance announcing that the project was financed in part by Europe. It spoke millions!

The main work areas for me were pipeline surveys and water/wastewater treatment. In pipeline surveys the physical condition of all properties along the pipeline route are photographically recorded, prior to work commencing; effectively insurance policies for the contractor. Pipeline surveys were done in Dublin, Enniscorthy, Kilkenny, Carlow, Wicklow Town, Bray, Dun Laoghaire and Killaloe. Pipeline surveys are measured in miles!

Water treatment, Leixlip, Co. Kildare

It was, however, in water and wastewater treatment that I travelled far: Belturbet, Dundalk, Leixlip, Ringsend, Lough Egish, Killeshandra, Enniscorthy, Donegal Town, Moville, Thurles, West Clare, Nenagh, Achill Island, Listowel, Inniscarra, Waterford, Drogheda, Ballymore Eustace, Swords, Kilkenny, Dun Laoghaire, Rathvilly, Bray and Wicklow Town.

Some standout events from my records: 1) survey: working in the River Dargle for eight days recording two miles of the river banks for flood control; 2) viewpoint: working from a cage suspended by a crane high above three water towers under construction in Sligo and Mullingar; 3) travel: to Bray and Wicklow Town, usually via the Sally Gap scenic route eighty-three times.

Panoramic Ireland, 11 June 1993
On the left: Mr. Lawrence Cassidy, The Arts Council,
who opened the exhibition

Landscape — a parallel world. In March 1989 I purchased a special camera, the first of its type sold by Linhof in the Republic. It was a serious piece of kit that greatly enhanced my work. It was a panoramic camera, making it eminently suited to photography of landscape. Over the years 1989–93 I made an extensive landscape collection from thirty counties. Armagh and Monaghan escaped this time. I made six trips to Northern Ireland, each of several days. Driving a Kildare-registered vehicle attracted the attention of the security forces every time, but never was a problem. I presented this work to state departments, semi-state and commercial companies. The Department of the Environment invited me to mount a display at their exhibition hall, ENFO, 17 St Andrew's Street. They had the facilities and a staff experienced in mounting exhibitions and arranging publicity. Here I hit the jackpot. Paddy made sixty large mounted prints. The exhibition ran for four weeks in midsummer 1993. The reviews were favourable, and the Bank of Ireland calendar — and much more besides — followed.

Much have I travelled in Ireland, and much have I seen, which has given me a knowledge of the country, its infrastructure and its landscape, which I claim to be quite unique. I made no fortune, but I had great freedom, and I loved every minute of it. How should I price that?

I brought my second career to an end in the late '90s. In December 2007, after an absence of 52 years, I returned to the Beara Peninsula, the place of my birth. Here I still occasionally wander up into the hills with a camera and a tripod, to once again record where the land meets the restless sea.

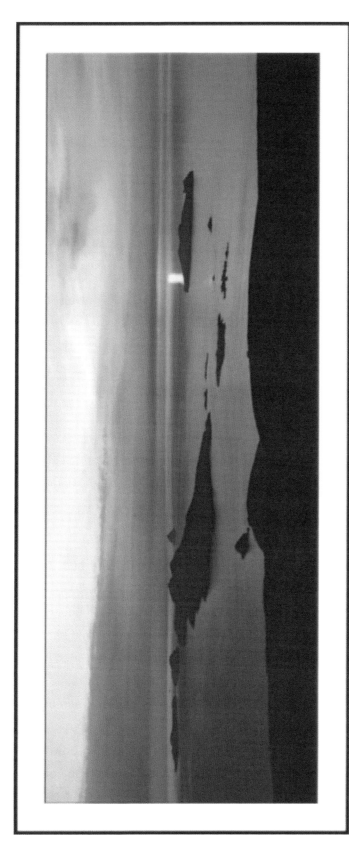

Like silent sentries in the Western Ocean
The Blasket Islands, Co. Kerry

A Proud Tradition

Jim Prendergast

Taken at 2/Lt John's Commissioning, 11 May 1992. Left to Right:
Lt Mark Prendergast, Member 63rd Cadet Class.
Pl Comdr 27th Inf Bn, Dundalk
Lt Gareth Prendergast, Member 65th Cadet Class.
Pl Comdr 29th Inf Bn, Monaghan
2/Lt John Prendergast, Member 67th Cadet Class.
Posted to 2 Fd Arty Regt, McKee Bks, Dublin
Lt Col Jim Prendergast, Member 35th Cadet Class.
Officer Commanding Magee Bks, Kildare.

Gloria and I were surprised that our three sons decided to make the army their career, and asked what motivated them. Their answer was that I was always happy in the army and the army was always held in high esteem in our home town in Mullingar.

There was a great relationship between the people of Mullingar and the Defence Forces. It was the policy that new officers should engage in local activities by joining clubs and community groups. An officer from Columb Barracks occupied a seat on the board of Mullingar Credit Union, the reason being that the representative on the board would look after the interests of army members of the credit union. After many years I became that board member.

Due to my involvement in the credit union I was asked by a number of NCOs and Gunners if I would help them to form a cooperative group that would enable them to build their own homes. It is very pleasing when one is asked for help so I agreed. At that time there was great government support for cooperative building groups. We registered our building society under the "Friendly Society Act" and I became the company secretary. As we know it may not be compliant with D.F.R. A7 to form a society in the army so we called ourselves "The Columb Barracks Building Group". Thankfully with generous grants and support from Westmeath Co. Council, we built seventeen bungalows for our members.

Similar to many of my classmates I served most of my time as a junior officer in the same unit. During that time our experiences were similar. Unit and barrack activities, an overseas trip to Cyprus. I commend my classmates who served with distinction on many overseas missions. The troubled situation that developed in the North of Ireland in 1969 brought new challenges with service on the border. The establishment of three new Infantry battalions and the improvement in our equipment to meet this new threat lifted morale and hastened our promotional prospects.

May I divert to share a funny experience with you. I was the orderly officer in Columb Barracks Mullingar on Sunday September 28th 1975 (which was during the height of the troubles) when I received a telephone call from the police in Manchester. The station sergeant informed me that they had a man in custody who claimed to be my commanding officer. As was the procedure at the time I received his telephone number and called him back. I described my commanding officer to the station sergeant who was satisfied that his guest was in fact my commanding officer. I apologised to the station sergeant for the inconvenience caused. He replied "do not worry we have dingbats at senior level in our force too".

On promotion to Comdt I was posted to the Command and Staff school in the Military College. This was a totally new experience which necessitated moving my family to Newbridge. I look back with great fondness at the experience I gained and the friends that I and my family made in the army and town of Newbridge.

Having served three years in the Command and Staff school I was posted back to Mullingar as "Regional Civil Defence Officer" for the counties of Longford, Westmeath Laois and Offaly. This was a new world where my boss was Assistant Secretary in the Department of Defence and my job was to promote Civil Defence in the four counties. I have great admiration for the members of the Civil Defence who give their time to the betterment of their communities. Members of the Civil Defence are volunteers who do not receive any payment for their time.

Back to the 4 Fd Arty Regt. as 2/ic and then, on to the Lebanon as 2/ic 63 Inf Bn.

December 1989 was the highlight of my career when I was promoted Lt. Col and appointed OC of my original unit the 4 Fd Arty unit.

I was promoted Colonel in 1996 which was an unexpected bonus.

Looking back it is little wonder that I enjoyed every day in the army. I thank God for the experience.

After my retirement I continued with my involvement in the credit union and the community council. These activities and interests enhance my quality of life right up to the present day.

In addition to my three sons Mark's wife Ciara Ware was a member of the defence forces who took early retirement with the rank of Commandant.

To date our family has given 160 years to the permanent defence forces.

Between Ireland and Croatia

Maurice Sweeney

Maurice with Paddy out fishing in Falcarragh, 1961

We are now approaching the 60th anniversary of the reporting by the members of the 35th Cadet Class to the Cadet School in the Military College.

At that time I would never have imagined that sixty years later I would be dividing my time between Ireland and the Republic of Croatia.

In 1961, Croatia was a member of the Socialist Federal Republic of Yugoslavia. The country had a history of conflict, when in the 9th century it became part of the Roman empire. In the 16th century, following Ottoman victories in the region, Croatia joined the Austrian-Hungarian empire for protection. In 1918 Croatia left the empire and merged with Serbia and Slovenia to form the Kingdom of Yugoslavia. In 1941 the axis invaded Yugoslavia. A Nazi-backed puppet state was formed and concentration camps were established to house Jews, Roma and Serbs. Up to 200,000 were killed. A communist anti-fascist resistance group was formed called the Yugoslav Partisan Movement, with Tito as its leader. This group was supported by the allies, and by May 1945 controlled all of Yugoslavia. After the death of Tito in 1980, the political situation in Yugoslavia deteriorated and in June 1991, following the independence of Slovenia, Croatia declared independence. By the end of 1991 an all-out conflict took place between Croatian forces, the Yugoslav People's Army (JNA) and Serb paramilitary groups. In January 1992 Croatia was recognised by the EEC and the UN. Both organisations sent multinational representatives, including Ireland. In August 1995 Croatia launched Operation Storm as part of the Homeland War, and forced Serbs out of four regions within Croatia. Croatia joined NATO in April 2009 and the EU in July 2013.

The President is the head of state, elected for a five year term. Croatia shares its borders with Slovenia, Hungary, Serbia, Bosnia-Herzegovina and Montenegro.To the west of the country is the Adriatic sea. The country has a population of four million, of which 86% are Catholic and 5% Orthodox. Croatia covers an area of 57,000 square kilometres. Croatian is the official language. The capital is Zagreb. Other cities/towns are Dubrovnik, Zadar, Split, Vukovar, Rijeka, Pula and Varazdin. The climate is continental with the warmest climate along the Adriatic coast.

Croatian built M-84A4 Battle tank

Croatian armed forces, which include the army, navy and air force, have a total strength of 21,000 with a reserve of 18,300. The annual budget is 718 million euro and is 1.3% of GDP. Conscription was abolished in 2008. The army has 650 AFVs,150 pieces of artillery, 100 MLRs and 70 tanks. The air force has 12 MiG 21 jet fighters, 10 combat transport aircraft and 16 attack helicopters. The navy has 29 ships. Croatian armed forces take part in NATO exercises and have 106 deployed to Afghanistan. In all 561 personnel are deployed between NATO and the UN. Croatia has developed an arms industry which exports upwards of 325 million euro.

In short, Croatia has an excellent climate, interesting places to visit and a cost of living lower than that of Ireland. It is very dependent on tourism and given the present circumstances regarding CoVid-19 it may suffer a recession.

Saighdiúir
David Taylor (1942–2016)

By Neil Taylor

For those of you who knew David Taylor, take some time to remember and reflect. Picture him on one of his best days, perhaps in uniform, maybe in command, competing on the rifle range or possibly diligently going about his duties. Allow yourself to smile and do not allow what Alzheimers stole from David taint your memory of him.

A question: Who was David Taylor and what did he represent? Well there were many names and titles which referred to him: Sir, Dáithí, Niner, Taylor, General, Davey, Herr Flick (a nickname born of his stoic Germanic nature and popular among his sons friends) and others no doubt. While he may have had a multiple of names, elevated rank, command and associated status, he never lost sight of who he really was and where he came from.

He was simply a proud son of Ireland, Connacht, Galway and Dominick Street, who epitomised the notion of 'Service before Self'. He was not proud in a bombastic or boastful way, but proud in the contentment and comfort of knowing who he was and what he represented. He represented with honour the soldierly attributes of endurance, perseverance, timeliness, loyalty, preparedness and selfless service.

"If I had eight hours to chop down a tree I would spend six hours sharpening the axe." The quoted words of Abraham Lincoln spring to mind when I think of him — constantly planning and preparing with the utmost precision.

He was loyal, decent, dedicated, dutiful, diligent, determined, direct, firm, fair and reservedly friendly. While he operated at a respectful distance, he was not remote; just deliberately removed and with a command of his emotions that he exercised with an iron will. Perhaps he was an unknowing advocate and ambassador of Genghis Khan's 'stone face' methodology, as practiced by Mongol warriors, where emotions were not betrayed by facial or physical expression and were mastered for a higher purpose. He was, for many, a role model whose professional and personal integrity remained firmly intact and whose word was, indeed, his bond.

He was in many ways a case study of self-discipline and iron will, who sought excellence in the vocational nature of his application to his professional, personal and social life. Aristotle is accredited with the following reference; "Excellence is an art won by habituation and training. We are what we repeatedly do. Excellence then, is not an act, but a habit." He sought to be in that habit and to occupy that space.

He was a man of few words and carefully constructed sentences who, when he chose to speak, delivered his message with the accuracy of a precision guided missile. Were you ever called to him with a beckoning finger or subject to the thousand-yard stare before being summoned for a chat? Anyone lucky enough to be invited to the office or indeed the dinner table, or some counsel understands how accurate, pointed and precise his guidance was. It was delivered to achieve maximum effect and rarely missed the target.

He had no airs or graces. He was who he was. To him everyone was equal, regardless of rank, origin or status. He held no favourites and as an officer saw himself simply as a soldier of higher rank. The saighdiúr singil was always at least as important as any other, in terms of how he exercised and practiced his duties. A product of a Jesuit education he was indeed a leader for others, never dwelling on the entitlements and benefits of title, status or rank but keenly feeling the responsibilities that such rank bestowed and taking a keen and deep interest in all those with whom he served.

He was not shallow, affected, self-servingly disingenuous or materialistic in any way. He truly was almost monastic in his existence, yet extremely generous in a quiet and unassuming way.

He had two real vocations in life; his family and the Defence Forces. He was very lucky to have had a supportive family and wonderful wife. Margaret, his 'oyster pearl', allowed him to be the man that he was. She was the bedrock of familial stability that allowed David to lead, to command, to mentor and to serve, secure in the knowledge that the needs of his family and indeed his own were always met.

Beyond his vocations he had some deep passions: sport, travel, theatre, food, music and song. He was fascinated by the psychology of competitive performance, whether it be in darts, rowing, soccer, golf or military marksmanship. All passions exercised him differently, some presenting him with challenges and others giving him great comfort and solace in their repetition. To hear him laugh uncontrollably at the Marx Brothers every Christmas brought tears of joy to the eyes of those who witnessed him at his most relaxed. The 'stone face' slipped on occasion, most notably when Frank Stapleton failed again to convert a chance for Ireland or Manchester United. His dietary discipline was compromised occasionally by a ninety-nine cone at the Druid Theatre interval, or by indulging in a Drimcong House dessert.

He took his passion for sport and shooting seriously, mirroring Gary Player's words that "the harder I practice the luckier I get". He loved the challenge and rewards that purposeful practice bestowed on him, whether as an individual or a team member. Hundreds, if not thousands, of hours were spent honing his crafts and seeking mastery of the three iron, the FN and indeed the Steyr AUG. However, he took equal joy from coaching, supporting and mentoring others, taking a deep satisfaction from seeing others develop, blossom and evolve positively under his tutelage. They all knew, as soldiers or sportsmen, that he would never demand of them anything which he hadn't already demanded repeatedly of himself.

He had a quiet but deep personal faith which he practiced discreetly. He practiced but didn't preach. Perhaps this faith, among other deeply-ingrained personal traits, helped him to endure, to drive on with determination and to remain resolute in the face of adversity, challenge and (at times) occasional conflict.

Footnote: Had he a regret, or if he had been in a position in his later years to express any regret, I suspect that it would be this; he felt that his command and leadership in south Lebanon, as OC 'C' Company in the village of At Tiri, should have been formally recognised by the organisation that he served with such dedication and distinction. No doubt he shouldered this burden of regret as something that he could not control nor remedy. It is perhaps ironic that he was regularly tasked with addressing officer career courses in the Curragh on the leadership lessons of At Tiri, knowing that his command there was considered a case study and model of leadership excellence, and yet no action was ever taken to publicly acknowledge the leadership delivered and service given.

Saighdiúir agus laoch ab ea é.

34th and 35th Class' visit to Bulmers Factory
Clonmel, 1961

Investigating Crimes of War

Experiences and Issues

Des Travers

War Crime Training

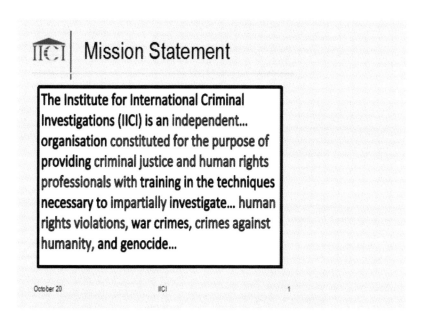

I became involved with the Institute for International Criminal Investigations (www.iici.global) in 2002, when asked by one of its founders, former Chief of Staff Lt Gen Gerry MacMahon, to present a module on their War Crime Investigator Course being held in The Hague. The Institute's inaugural course had been held the previous year at the Irish Centre for Human Rights, ICHR, UCG, Galway.

I was invited to sit in on the other subjects being taught there. The international law aspect was being taught by Dr — now Professor — Ray Murphy who served as a Captain in the Defence Forces before joining ICHR. He has delivered the international law module to IICI investigator courses since.

I found the subjects fascinating, in particular the International Law module. What occurred to me was the apparently seamless extension of past peacekeeping experience, especially in the operations and information sphere, with that of present war crime investigation methods. I say 'apparently', as over the years I had to acquire a considerable number of methods and procedures skills that are required by the investigation system. In addition, one had to absorb accretions of the investigation culture where some on occasion appeared antagonistic to militaries; all militaries at that.

IICI, just recently established, was the first such institute devoted to training in war crime investigation. Over time this training expanded to providing advice and consultancies to organisations and individuals involved in such investigations. This arose, in the main, because board members and instructors had developed their skills in recent war crime investigations, in particular at the International Criminal Tribunal on the Former Yugoslavia, ICTY. Attendees on IICI courses were required to be qualified and practicing in their respective fields; police, lawyers, analysts, forensic scientists and human rights specialists. The laws and methods governing investigations, evidence-gathering and witness-interviewing would of course be different from one jurisdiction to another. IICI's Investigator Course mission was to train practitioners in the specifics of investigations that would be acceptable at international level.

The military module concerned itself with military organisation, tactics, equipment, recognition aids (fighting vehicles, weapons, uniforms and rank markings). Its purpose was to assist investigators in determining which belligerent was likely to have committed the crime under investigation.

It further helped to assist with making determinations arising from a doctrine known as Command Responsibility. Command Responsibility is unique and approximates to the governance by a ship's captain at sea when outside all other jurisdictions. In essence, a commander is deemed responsible for everything his/her unit does or fails to do. Quite fortuitously this responsibility agrees with well understood obligations of military command taught in military academies the world over; "...*you are responsible for everything your unit does or fails to do.*" This means the commander can be indicted even if he/she did not commit the crime or was elsewhere, for example on leave, during the commission of the incident under investigation.

Command Responsibility is one of the great determinants of guilt or innocence in the war crimes area. Since the former Yugoslav conflict and ICTY's subsequent indictments, it had been noticed that commanders more frequently defer to their legal officers before embarking on a military operation. This is a positive step. Indeed in one proposed coalition enterprise involving military operations against another country, the military leadership advised their political superiors that they would not be prepared to commit without a legal instrument justifying such actions. As one General opined, "...we do not want to spend our years of retirement in a jail somewhere...!"

Sexual and Gender-Based Violence (SGBV)

Over the years since Nuremberg, the ongoing development of human rights has given rise to the inclusion of areas of crime that hitherto had been considered 'nuisances' committed by soldiery — such as rape and pillage — and now has created a code under the acronym SGBV. It does surprise this student of military history that some western armies during WWII committed greater levels of rape and plunder on liberated people than the retreating axis army of occupation.

While SGBV is relatively new, it does in its gender formulations include sexual crimes against males. It is considered that 40% of all crimes of a sexual nature in war are crimes against males. In discussing this aspect I am not intending here to minimize in any way such crimes against females, nor especially children. However, in my view this 40% figure may be an under-estimation and for understandable reasons. There is a known disinclination in male victims to report such crimes. Indeed in recent conflicts such incidents were only later reported by spouses or partners when they noted behavioral changes in their male partners. There is also the bizarre situation where HR organisations devoted to assisting victims of sexual violence, were not disposed or resourced to assist male victims!

Added to this must be the fact that such crimes in some forty-six jurisdictions are considered to be grave crimes that not only criminalise perpetrators but also their victims. In some of these jurisdictions it is a capital offence to have carried out or participated in such acts.

Finally on the SGBV issue may I offer the comment that sexual crimes by males against males are crimes committed by *heterosexuals*.

Soldier Investigates Soldier

Over the course of the almost two decades with IICI, I have been asked by alumni for answers to military-specific questions that have arisen in their investigations. These questions have come from nearly all the known areas of conflict: Libya, Syria, Sudan, Afghanistan and the Occupied Palestinian Territories. I have welcomed these questions as they hone my competencies in the military analysis area. I should also mention that where questions arise about new defence technologies or *materiel de guerre* since my peacekeeping days, I have fallen back on the Ordnance Corps School, Curragh for their technical inputs. I owe them a debt of gratitude, especially to the School Commandant and his staff for their helpfulness at all times.

These requests for opinions later developed into participation in investigations such as:

- Membership of a UN Fact Finding Mission, whose finding came to be known as the 'Goldstone Report'.
- Consultant military analyst with various enquiries, such as the Sri-Lankan–Tamil War (2009) and military crimes during martial law in Bolivia (2002).
- Tutor and interpreter of military events with international law students, in Gaza and at Harvard, and so on.

In addition, I have had to defend my work and that of my colleagues and our findings in distinguished forums such as: UNHCHR, Geneva, the Dáil (foreign affairs committee on three occasions); the European Union; the French Senate; the House of Lords; Liberal-Democratic conference, UK, and academies such as Harvard, Boston College, LSE London, American University of Beirut and several UK and Irish universities.

A cartoon of Des Travers delivering a talk on the
Goldstone Report in Brussels.

These investigations of recent conflicts occurred across four continents and allow me the opportunity to offer some generalisations about such conflicts.

But first, may I offer a comment about a word that hops in and out of the lexicon of insurgency warfare and is of concern to me. It is the word 'terrorist'. I have come across some twelve definitions of it, none of which are satisfactory nor seem to recognise the original reason and meaning for the term, and some of which infer a violent person not of the Judeo-Christian tradition. The use of the word is so self-serving that it prejudices the user, in my view.

I did however hear of a definition from a police friend that isn't at all bad if it came to be the internationally agreed one. It is this: "…a terrorist is a person who resorts to violence in pursuit of an ideology…" His full definition included, "… when non-violent means are available to achieve his ideological ends". I reject this addendum because it de-legitimises some 'terrorists' I know, including those who fought for our independence.

The majority of the conflicts that I have observed are conflicts of states pitted against elements within that state or in disputed segments within and/or adjacent to that state. Invariably this comes down to the armed forces of the state in conflict with dissident elements whose conflict capabilities are often improvisational in nature. War crimes will usually be committed by both sides. Indeed I know of no conflict in which a belligerent was free from war crime or human rights violations. I have however noticed that the preponderance of war crimes are committed by the larger force, that is the armed forces of the state. These crimes occur frequently when the armed force in question has the upper hand or when it has moved to the final phase of the conflict.

Put in another way, war crime is committed by those who have the wherewithal to do it and the opportunity to do so. It has nothing to do with 'contributing to the mission of the armed force', 'ethnic cleansing' or some other strategy.

Similarly I wish to debunk the notion of 'rape warfare' as a facet of conflict, with the exception of where there is genocidal intent. Otherwise rape is rape. Period. It has nothing to do with any tactic or strategy and is opportunist in nature. Indeed experts in the field I work with, suggest three criteria for rape to occur in conflict. These are:

- [Soldiers'] *time* away from home,
- [Soldiers'] *distance* from home and
- *Opportunity*.

Needless to say that these conditions determine behavior regardless of the race, colour, religious belief or discipline of those troops.

The *opportunity* aspect of rape is of interest. For example, forward combat troops are less likely to commit such crimes while support troops in the rear are more likely to do so. Where it has been made a court-martial (or a dismissal in the case of officers) offence to permit non-combatants, male or female, to come close to a post or defended area, the opportunity aspect seems to have been addressed. This has arisen with IDF troops in engagements in Gaza. However this has produced an increase in unlawful killings of persons, often on the basis that they may be suicide bombers.

Inappropriate Munitions

Many weapons of various kinds in use today are unethical in my view, and ought to be unlawful also. That said, I have yet to observe any human rights organisation of repute take issue about their use or their manufacture. This concern arises especially when the weapon — or more correctly, the munition — in question has been in long term use (misuse?) in many instances since the Cold War or earlier. There seems to be an ambivalence about their manufacture and about their deployment. If they are manufactured in the west giving employment and exports — that's okay. If they are being used in a far off trouble-spot, '...*East of Suez*...' — well, that's ok too.

Some of these somewhat old reliables merit mention. The first is the highly effective illuminant chemical white-phosphorus (WP). Its use in signaling, especially distress signaling, is well known. However, in munitions — especially when air-dropped over a densely populated area — their use becomes problematic. This is especially so since WP as a chemical is toxic and highly volatile. Particles of WP may re-ignite sometime days or weeks after discharge; it burns human and animal tissue to the bone; when undergoing treatment or removal can reignite and can in turn cause sickness and nausea in medical teams treating patients with such burns. Finally, one professor of medicine observed that those he treated with relatively survivable WP burns, died. He opined that the cause of death was a form of 'toxic shock'.

To test his theory the professor was going to send tissue samples back to his university in Europe for analyses.

I failed to tell him it would be a waste of time.

Air burst WP over Gaza, Jan 2009

Incapacitation

"This grenade is guaranteed not to kill."

(Salesperson to author)

The 'fashionable' idea of incapacitation as the more acceptable option (as opposed to killing) now needs a re-examination, in my view. If incapacitation means permanent or long-term incapacitation then we have a human rights issue crying out for attention. Some examples and their consequences may be worth flagging:

- Firing a high velocity round at the lower extremities of a protester seems acceptable until one considers the full consequences, not only to the victim but to the society that must care for that victim. Such a round will turn bone into 'biological shrapnel' thereby inflicting serious wounding. This has a multiplier effect in a blockaded economy with limited resources and even more limited medical amenities. It has been suggested elsewhere that an incapacitated person adds a fivefold burden to the community that must care for such a victim.

- Flechettes, metal darts 50mm in length and fired in salvo from a tank shell, seem to be an appropriate anti-personnel measure. However the design and velocity of the flechette is so determined that it tumbles when coming in contact with flesh, thereby creating significant internal injuries. It is a concern to this writer that one manufacturer in its promotional literature states that their flechettes are designed to 'tumble' on impact. In my view this makes the flechette a dum-dum projectile. Due to the salvo effect (there are 1,800 flechettes in a tank shell) if a victim is within range he/she will usually be struck by more than one flechette. Several impacts should, in my view, produce incapacitation without the need for an evisceration effect due to 'tumbling'.

All the aforementioned are low-end munitions in the modern military arsenal. They should and could be corrected at relatively little cost and with little tactical consequence. But first, appropriate international agencies and human rights organisations might be prompted to address these issues.

They should take heart from the Dublin Moratorium of 2008 on the use of cluster bombs. At this conference one hundred and eight (108) countries signed the moratorium. This need arose when some 400,000 cluster bombs were dropped over South Lebanon during the Hisb'Allah conflict of 2006. Designed to explode on impact, a suspiciously high number of them, estimated at 40%, failed to do so. Previous use by the same armed force had a failure rate of 18%. Those that did not explode on impact became anti-personnel mines.

Irish Peacekeepers recall farmers lifting them with their shovels and stockpiling them on field edges. "I have to clear my field. I have to feed my family," one farmer said, when told of the risks he was taking.

"Mowing the Lawn"

(General's euphemism for neutralising urban areas by bombing.)

If incapacitation is an issue at the lower end of the military spectrum, what of the 'precision munitions' at the upper end? In my view this aspect requires attention.

A micro-shrapnel sleeve fitted to Hellfire missiles killed some eighty-eight (88) policemen at a graduation ceremony in Gaza. Micro-shrapnel as opposed to DIME (Dense Inert Metal Explosive) munitions are 3–4mm cubes of tungsten. Their purpose, it is to be assumed, is to optimise lethality in exchange for such an effect being confined to a limited radius.

This gives rise to the question of weapon adaptations and their subsequent testing against live targets. Such flagrant use also suggests a means to demonstrate the lethality of the adaptation to developers.

Precision munitions that I have observed were intended to engage single targets for a specified end or area targets when used for assumed tactical purposes.

The single target engagement was frequently observed in the several conflicts in the Middle East. The munition being used was usually a conventional cold war era high explosive (HE) bomb with a 500kg payload. It was, however, fitted with a GPS guidance system and a delay-action fuse. It was a low-cost upgrade at $10,000 (at 2005 prices) and proved to be highly cost-effective.

Fired or launched at an apartment building the bomb, usually a JDAM Mk 82 (Joint Direct Attack Munition, Mark 82), would penetrate the roof and all floors before detonating in the basement. The basement confined the energy of the explosion; the area of least resistance was upwards; the bomb's energy tearing through the structure's interior, its most vulnerable area. A building thus impacted would collapse inward crushing all inside. Buildings adjacent to it would be unscathed.

In some instances the building did not collapse immediately but did so later or was caused to do so by rescue teams. The horrific thought of entombment came to mind when witnessing a recovery team searching the rubble of a partially collapsed apartment in Saida (Sidon, July 2006) when it was known that a mother and her two daughters were trapped inside. When found they were lying side by side covered in dust and debris and did not seem to show injuries. They most likely suffocated.

Do not do this at home! Unexploded JDAM, S. Lebanon, July 2006

On occasion a building resisting such an impact may stand for a moment. Then like some prehistoric beast, creak and collapse.

As a former soldier one has to grudgingly admire the ruthless efficiency of such target elimination. There are two issues that arise from it; excessive use and reprisal response.

The excessive use issue arises when an attack is analysed. Such attacks were occasioned, according to spokespersons, when the building was a known residence of a resistance leader or was a place known to be a sniper position, or seemingly to deny the building to a sniper or observer. If one were to put such a rationale into tactical-speak, It seems to be the denial of key terrain to the enemy, by *eliminating* it. This seems to me to be a step beyond the original intent of controlling or dominating key terrain.

The use of precision bombing is another matter. In one incident in which a number of JDAM were used, it was intended as a warning and a reprisal against an ethnic or religious community. The community, mainly Shia from south Lebanon, resided in a complex of apartments in southern Beirut and were perceived to be sympathetic to the Hisb'Allah movement. The district Dahiya gave rise to a doctrine of 'excessive response'. It was intended, according to this Dahiya doctrine, to produce a 'lasting response' in the minds of its victims.

Weapons Testing and Marketing

In the course of my military analysis experience one issue above all others that calls for attention is that of weapons testing. By 'weapons testing' I include new weapons or systems that are ushered into a conflict for marketing purposes. In my estimation I have encountered at least four test/marketing munitions incidents. These are: the previously mentioned micro-shrapnel incident; the use of a mine-clearing munition (called Carpet) in a suburban area; the use of a thermobaric or fuel-air bomb in a basement; and the use of a new indirect firing weapon into a crowded street.

It is not at all unusual for weapons manufacturers to usher their products into a war zone so that they can be marketed as 'war tested'. Where this becomes very problematic is when the 'war' itself is deemed unlawful and where the 'targets' for the weapons trial are indiscriminate or are non-combatants.

One weapons trial sets the scene for all that is wrong with unrestricted development and marketing of defence materiel. The test involved an indirect fire weapon known as Keshet whose systems had been automated. The target was a market street on a busy market day. The street was not accessible to other conventional indirect fire weapons as buildings on both sides would 'trap' the descent of artillery shells.

Automatic Mortar

Drones hovered overhead to capture the shoot. The shoot involved firing bombs along the street at such short intervals that those targeted would be frozen or unable to respond or flee towards the next impact further along the street.

Three impacts each necessitated rapid adjustment to sights and gun alignment so employed. The shoot accounted for over thirty fatalities and a similar number of serious wounded, not to mention killing of livestock and destruction of farm produce.

Spokespersons justifying this attack stated that it was an attack on terrorists. It was noted that among the 'terrorists' they listed was a thirteen year old boy.

A kafkaesque quandary seeps into the human rights investigation field — and especially so the medical care communities — when they catalogue the consequences of this action. Their information is what the weapons testers need; it confirms or proves the lethality of their product and is available at no cost to them in receiving it. Moreover this is data that cannot be replicated in a range or lawful test facility.

In effect it pays to test weapons or market them in an area of conflict, so called. Weapons manufacturers will continue to do so until some measures are put in place to prevent them from doing it.

Depleted Uranium (DU)

I became concerned by this next and last munition when it was used very surgically to destroy border tunnel systems in a recent conflict. The munitions used had been imported as a one-off initiative from a major western manufactory.

After the bombing, military engineers removed the soil over the impact sites to a depth of about six feet, and then replaced it with fresh soil brought in from elsewhere. The implications of this last event are obvious.

Not so obvious to some technical colleagues however are the hazards associated with DU, if not at the user end then perhaps at the impact site. As a debating point, the DU issue produces an overlap between science and conspiracy theory; users and victims; guns and targets; and so on. Suffice it to suggest that our duty of care to soldiers as peacekeepers require us to have due consideration in committing them to a mission in which DU munitions have been used. At least one government thought so, and withdrew their peacekeepers. Without explanation.

Media and Modern War Crime

Modern technologies that have created and influenced social media have also entered the military sphere. In the past during my peacekeeping days, analyses of incidents were often relatively uncomplicated. An incident was to be investigated; an impact site or crater was examined; witnesses, if any, were interviewed; a determination as to who the perpetrator may be was arrived at. If the impact or house-blowing had certain characteristics and debris it was usually possible to make a determination as to who was the perpetrator and why. If, for example, the impact and debris revealed a projectile of Soviet origin, say a Katyusha rocket, then it could be assumed it was fired by a Palestinian or Islamic element — whichever was in the ascendent in Lebanon at that time.

Similarly if the impact site was a crater and the crater's configuration and its debris indicated a HE shell of 155mm calibre that came from a gun-position south east of there, then it could be assumed that it was fired by an IDF artillery battery or by their proxy the LAUI (Lebanese Armed and Uniformed by Israel) of Maj. Saad Haddad.

Blowing up of houses, tit-for-tat and often caused by family feuds, could also be analysed and reliable findings made. And so on.

In recent years complications have arisen in the investigation sphere. This arises especially where incidents were likely to have been caused by government forces, forces that have the back-up resources to manage and manipulate the media. In one example, refugees fled into 'no-fire-zones' and were subsequently shelled by the creators of those zones. Requests to conduct crater analyses in those zones, in order to determine the perpetrators, was refused by the Sri Lankan authorities. In some cases an incident which had been captured by video has caused other unspecified agencies to be able to produce videos which tell an opposite story. Such forms of attack and the doctrine that underpins it have rightly been deemed unlawful in the various findings in which this matter is discussed. In some cases an incident which had been captured by video has caused other unspecified agencies to be able to produce videos which tell an opposite story.

In this case the services of a public relations firm based in the UK was hired to manufacture and manage misinformation. This they did quite effectively. This is to my mind aiding and abetting and should be treated accordingly.

The attack on the freedom flotilla vessel the MV Marmara on the high seas in 2010 is one such case. Videos were produced which seemed to show crew and passengers beating with belaying pins the IDF soldiers who had rappelled on board from helicopters.

Another example which is a concern relates to the disclosure of videos by Sri Lankan army personnel. In them are scenes of the naked bodies of young Tamil women laid out in a row while Sri Lankan soldiers walked among them making lewd or derogatory comments about them. Later videos show these bodies being dragged by the heels and dumped into military trucks. Blurred versions of these videos are available to view on YouTube. The unblurred videos are much more disturbing.

Shelling of No-Fire zones, Sri Lanka, 2009

The blurring of these grim scenes may mollify the squeamish. They also serve the interests of the perpetrators. They do so by diminishing the horror of these crimes for the viewer. They permit low cost 'fake' videos of similar scenes but where the 'soldiers' portrayed in them are speaking Tamil! Even obvious fakes induce doubt as to the veracity of the originals. That is sufficient in itself.

The war crimes known or suspected to have occurred during the closing days of the Sri Lankan-Tamil war which occurred during the early months of 2009 have not been subject to trial by the international community. There are various reasons for this which I do not intend to discuss here as they are non-analysis issues.

However there is one aspect to the reason for this 'failure' that merits comment. This is the presumption of impunity; some western states and some non-western allies seem to enjoy it for various reasons. Impunity, like power, corrupts. This corruption occurs in the investigative sphere when third tier expertise is needed as part of an investigation. Briefly, if forensic analysis of a piece of evidence were to be sought which may implicate entities of the impunitocracy then a negative outcome is likely. That or the evidence sample gets 'lost' in the post!

I mentioned this to a senior government forensic scientist. He suggested that I should conceal the origin of the debris samples being offered for analysis. I think he missed the point I was trying to make.

Effects of past misdeeds

A lookback at these conflicts is merited. A significant number of them arise from ethnic or cultural impositions or the prioritisation of minorities by colonial powers. These left a heritage of discord in their wake. Oftentimes such realignments were done for both economic and divisive reasons by the colonial power in question. They continue to be issues today. It is my opinion that the history of colonialism in any one case cannot be fully tallied until a century has elapsed post-colonialism.

The democratic world has been the dominant entity in the ongoing development of human rights and crimes against humanity. Many of our more successful democracies were colonial powers in the past. Sometimes the spectre of that past seems to invade events in the present. Put another way, the Nuremberg trials have been criticised as 'victors' justice'. Its modern variant seems to have segued into 'westernised justice'.

By all accounts democracy is undergoing new challenges, both internally and externally. Recession circumstances have fueled the fire and we see a growing disinclination to engage with the plight of others. Europe's seemingly growing indifference to the influx of refugees is a case in point.

No one could have anticipated a slamming of doors of such intensity as that of a Secretary of State of the world's greatest democratic power's message to the President of the International Criminal Court when he wrote:

> "...Dear Madame Prosecutor,
> You are dead to us.
> Sincerely..."

Yes we have progressed.
Now we have to be watchful.

Des with a St Flannan's classmate!

United Nations Iraq-Kuwait Observation Mission
(UNIKOM)

John Vize

Introduction

Due to editorial constraints, what follows is a very brief broad outline of the UNIKOM mission. I will, therefore, confine my remarks to the more important aspects of the mission. I served as force commander from November 1999 to November 2001.

Background

On 2nd August 1990, Iraq invaded Kuwait and the international community reacted swiftly. The United Nations Security Council (UNSC) adopted resolution 660 condemning the invasion, and demanded Iraqi withdrawal of its forces. Iraq continued its occupation. On 16th January 1991 the UNSC authorised military operations which continued until late February, the first Gulf War.

On 3rd April 1991, the UNSC adopted resolution 687 which, among other things, provided for a DMZ along the Iraq-Kuwait border and UNIKOM was established.

The DMZ was two hundred and ten miles long, fifteen miles deep, ten miles on the Iraq side and five miles on the Kuwait side.

Mandate

To monitor the DMZ and waterway between both countries to deter violations through its presence in and surveillance of the DMZ.

Concept of Operations

This was based on a combination of patrol and observation based (POBs), ground and air patrols, investigation teams and liaison at all levels, including both ministries of foreign affairs of host countries. Every two months, I visited Baghdad and Kuwait city, accompanied by my senior political advisor, for discussions with senior political and military officers. We were always well received on these occasions.

Organisation

The DMZ was divided into 3 sectors, i.e. north, south and maritime, the latter being established during my tour of duty. This was an interesting exercise. (See appendices 1 & 2)

Member States' Participation

The participation, for the first time in the peace-keeping organisation (PKO) of all five permanent members of the security council, was an illustration of the international community's commitment to ensure the inviolability of the border area. An officer of the rank of Colonel from each of the permanent member (P5) countries held key appointments.

Situation in the DMZ

A. The situation in UNIKOM remained generally calm and quiet throughout my entire tour of duty. The number of incidents and incursions gradually decreased, mainly due to constant patrolling by land, air and sea by UNIKOM as well as the frequent liaison meetings, held with host nations at various levels.

B. Air violations of the DMZ mostly involved aircraft flying too high to be identified. Those that could be occasionally identified flew from the south to the north and were identified as aircraft used by the coalition forces.

C. Maritime violations involved patrol vessels or fishing boats of the state parties in each other's territorial waters. UNIKOM had two patrol boats.

D. The border security arrangements put in place by Kuwait — the trench, berm and wire fence — helped to reduce illegal cross-border activities.

E. Following the Gulf War, minefields on the Iraq side remained largely uncleared. Iraqi civilians became casualties while tending their flocks or searching for truffles and scrap metal in the desert. There were thirty-two casevacs in the year 2000 to German medical teams (GERMED) by heli and road, some fatal.

F. Following the events of 9/11 in the USA, the UNIKOM evacuation plan was revised and updated. It was to be used at a later date, prior to the second Gulf War.

Conclusion

A. My tour of duty as force commander was an immensely rewarding and satisfying 2 year period during which the mission continued to fulfil its mandate.

   This was achieved through the professionalism and dedication of the joint military/civilian teams and the unstinting endeavours of the UNMOS.

B. At times, my relationship with UNIKOM civilian management was less than fluent. The arbitrary imposition of some administrative measures, supposedly to counter perceived shortcomings in UNIKOM and which impinged on the conditions of service of the UNMOS, often without prior consultation with the force commander, was a source of deep frustration.

   There was only one visit by the department of peacekeeping operations (DPKO) to UNIKOM in my two year tour of duty.

C. I was most impressed with the professionalism of the Irish UNMOS with whom I had the pleasure to serve in the mission. In this regard, it was a privilege to work with our classmate, Colonel John Murray, who joined the mission as chief military personnel officer on his second tour of duty with UNIKOM.

D. Finally, I remain extremely grateful to DFHQ for the opportunity to have served as Force Commander UNIKOM.

Appendix (1)

Overview of the DMZ stretching from the Saudi Arabian border in the southwest to the Khawr Abd Allah waterway in the east, 210 km of land and 40 km of sea.

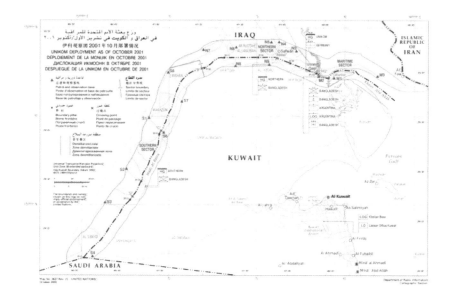

Appendix (2)

UNIKOM Organisational Structure

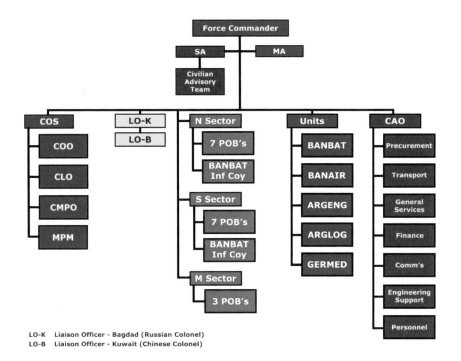

LO-K   Liaison Officer - Bagdad (Russian Colonel)
LO-B   Liaison Officer - Kuwait (Chinese Colonel)

Appendix (3)

Composition and strength of UNIKOM

MILITARY OBSERVERS			
Argentina	4	Malaysia	6
Austria	2	Nigeria	5
Bangladesh	6	Pakistan	6
Canada	5	Poland	6
China	11	Romania	5
Denmark	5	Russian Federation	11
Fiji	7	Senegal	5
Finland	5	Singapore	5
France	11	Sweden	5
Ghana	6	Thailand	5
Greece	4	Turkey	6
Hungary	6	United Kingdom	11
India	6	United States Of Amercia	11
Indonesia	6	Uruguay	6
Ireland	6	Venezueles	3
Italy	6		
Kenya	3	TOTAL	195

Military Support Units	
Bangladesh Mechanized Infantry Battalion (BANBAT)	775
Argentinean Engineer Unit (ARGENG)	50
Argentinean Logistics Group (ARGLOG)	30
Bangladesh Air Force Detachment (BANAIR)	35
German Medical Unit (GERMED)	14
TOTAL Military Support Units	904

TOTAL MILITARY PERSONNEL	1,099

Civilian Personnel	
International Staff	53
Locally Recruited Staff	146

TOTAL CIVILIAN PERSONNEL	199

Becoming a Cadet

Paddy Walshe

At about 10 am on 31ˢᵗ January 1961 I got on a CIE bus at Molly Barry's Cross near Kilworth with a one way ticket to the Curragh Camp. At about 11pm the night before I had made the last connection on Ireland's first Water Group Scheme in my home townland of Kilally. In June the previous year I had agreed to a request from my dad to take over the supervisory responsibility for the execution of the local water scheme, which was designed to supply water to thirty householders and also to thirteen farms. I had finished the Leaving Certificate and my dad advised me that this would be the most important thing I would ever do in my life.

With daily work parties from the area we worked seven days a week excavating one-metre-deep trenches for laying the mains piping of two, four and six inches in diameter. The branch lines consisted of one and a half inch and one inch piping for connecting to houses and farms. Very heavy persistent rain in the autumn and the beginning of winter caused serious damage to the trenching and added a huge amount to the efforts required to lay the piping. Working each day from early morning until dusk we managed to get all piping laid and fitted with heavy cast-iron sluice valves, gate valves and stopcocks, and on the western section several pressure-reducing valves. It was Ireland's first group water scheme and sixty years later it continues to function as planned.

I was glad to get on that bus to the Curragh. At Littleton a hurley-wielding passenger boarded and proceeded past me to the rear of the bus. On arrival at the Curragh I discovered that the man with the hurley was Larry Kiely of the Tipperary hurling team. Eddie Heskin may have been on that bus also.

June, 1960. First meeting of the group water scheme officials. Photograph of Paddy Walshe, Secretary and work supervisor, Michael Walshe, senior chairman and Patrick O'Brien, farmers representative.

My time in the Cadet School was not as difficult as I had expected, having spent years helping to milk sixteen cows every morning and every evening, and in particular the almost eight months of virtual slavery supervising the construction of the water scheme with its six miles of piping.

In the mid-afternoon of the 31st January the first parade of the 35th Cadet Class was taken by our Company Sergeant, M O'Duibhir (An Bualtain) before he marched us off to be issued with uniforms. He checked the class nominal roll and discovered that one cadet was missing, which had An Bualtain strutting up and down shouting again and again "An dalta Di Bheirlinn, ca bhfuil sí?"

At about 8pm on that first night, I decided that I would try on my new uniform. I went to the mirror in the washroom to adjust the collar and when I saw myself in this strange outfit I was so taken aback that I had to return to Gasra 3 and sit on my bed for a while. These are my abiding memories of my first day as a Cadet.

The Beginnings of a Lifelong Interest in Photography

Paddy Walshe

In 1952, on my tenth birthday, I bought my first camera from the proceeds of 24 rabbit snares I set on our farm and on the neighbouring farm of Pat Heskin (cousins of classmate Eddie from the other side of the Blackwater). I sold the rabbits on the way to school to a man in a van in Kilworth. In 1950 one rabbit earned between two shillings and half a crown. In 1953 the Myxomatosis virus was introduced into Ireland from Australia to control the rampant rabbit population and in less than a year the market for rabbits had collapsed; but not before I had made sufficient money to buy the camera and also a Raleigh fixed gear racing bike. The camera was a Braun Nurenberg twin lens reflex.

My next advance in photography was thanks to fellow Cadet Eugene Lavelle who had much more technical knowledge of cameras than I had. He advised me to purchase a Yashica twin lens reflex.

Capt Tom Gunn of the 2nd Regt. Artillery FCA (who was also a senior executive with the Agfa Gevaert Company) visited the Cadet School on several occasions and advised us on photography in general. Between 1962 and 1967 he taught me the rudiments of film processing and the relationship between contrast and density. In early 1967, he arranged for me to join an advanced course at his company's academy in Antwerp by vouching for my standing as a 'professional film processor'. There I received a high-grade qualification in the evaluation of colour related to the processing of colour films and prints.

The qualification I received, in thanks to Capt Tom Gunn, proved vital at the end of January 1983 when I was awarded a very prestigious contract just as I was retiring from the Army.

Historical Maps and NASA

The map store in Magee Barracks stored several tons of old 1:25000 maps of all 32 counties. The whole country was covered by about 720 different sheets. The maps were not on any map account and were from the 1800s with many archaeological details that were missing from subsequent editions. The British Army had used them as artillery maps. Over the years the many thousands of maps had got completely mixed up. With the help of the staff from the Artillery School, Dublin Universities and the Royal Hibernian Academy, I led a project that spanned three years sorting the maps until we got about 12 complete sets together.

In 1982, I provided a full set of these maps to the Geography Department of Trinity College Dublin. At the end of January 1983, Professor Adrian Phillips of the Geography/Geology Departments invited me to lunch with some other senior members of staff to thank me for the valuable map set. During lunch I told him that I was retiring from the Army the following week (6th February 1983). He asked what I was going to do when I retired, and I told him that I had a qualification from Antwerp on colour evaluation and colour processing. He told me that during the previous week they had signed the contract with NASA for access to their Landsat imagery for analysing gold bearing areas throughout the world. He had been wondering who they would get to print them and asked if this was something that I could do. I confirmed that this was the qualification I held and would just need to get more specialised gear to handle the NASA images. I was also cleared for security, having been an officer in the Defence Forces, with the assurance that no other person would have access to the imagery. Security of the images was a sensitive requirement. Up to that time such imagery was produced in state facilities in Karuna (Sweden), Farnborough (UK), Marseilles (France), and Los Angeles (USA). That is how I got the contract which would last for over 15 years.

My part in the scheme was the production of false colour maps in various sizes from 4 ft by 4ft square to 7ft by 9ft with a required scale accuracy of 0.5mm over the 9-foot dimension. The false colour maps required a critically accurate colour balance.

The contract entailed that I equip myself with a 10 inch by 10 inch square horizontal enlarger which ran on a 25-foot-long light rail system. It was built for me by the British De Vere Company. I had to extend the darkroom into one of the downstairs bedrooms as the enlarger was almost half the size of a JCB. It was a very expensive item.

Paddy Walshe,
Founder and MD

For over 15 years I produced mapping for exploration companies involved in gold mining operations from South America through Mexico to mainland USA and for several areas in Australia and in Indonesia. (Within a year of providing the exploration mapping for Irian Jawa in New Guinea, hordes of wild men attacked the exploration site with machetes and bows and arrows.) Specialist geologists accompanied the multiple maps to their destination to brief the exploration companies on their significance. The images were constructed from various elements of the visible spectrum extending into the invisible elements of ultraviolet and deep infra-red. One project was intended to identify water resources deep under the Southern Sahara, and in later stages the remote sensing imagery mapping was used to identify areas bearing rare earths for the emerging digital industry.

Infiltrado Communista

Paddy Walshe

On the 9th of September 1966, Mick Hartnett and myself availed of 6 weeks leave to help crew a 40ft ketch of over 16 tons displacement, 'The Richard', from Cork Harbour to Alicante along with Denis Murphy, chairman of the Cork Harbour Commissioners. The owner skipper was Dermot Kennedy from West Cork. We departed the Quayside in Cobh at 9pm and sailed beyond the Daunt Rock Lightship and set a course for the Scilly Islands. Mick decided to reset the ship's compass as we were leaving Cork Harbour which proved an unhelpful event. We missed the Scilly Islands and reached the coast of Devon where we tried to recalculate our new bearing to the Scilly Islands which were less than 25 miles from Land's End. Again, we missed the Scillies and had to turn back on our sailing route and eventually found them after midnight on our second day. The rest of the trip was easier because we were able to follow the light from the Ushant Lighthouse at the tip of Brittany.

In the Port of Brest we loaded provisions for the rest of the trip and proceeded down the coast of France and landed at Belle-Ile over a day later. After that we visited La Rochelle. The Harbour Authorities came to our boat, amazingly, enquiring what nationality our flag represented as they had no record of it in their documentation. From there we headed more or less West intending to by-pass the North coast of Spain. After two days, we decided that we weren't sure where we were, so we turned due south and eventually entered the little harbour at Dijon, west of San Sebastien.

The Harbour Police came to check us and were curious that our passports said Army Officer and they couldn't understand why the two of us (with beards at this stage) were dressed in kilts and furry hats. Franco had given instructions that any suspicious craft attempting to enter any harbour on the North Coast of Spain should be refused entry. The Police accused us of being Infiltrado Communista and instructed us to leave without delay. We departed Dijon and landed in the small port of Tapia farther west. There we were met by what appeared to be one of Franco's security operatives. We were allowed to land, but this old gentleman accompanied us wherever we went, including to a restaurant where we had a meal and some beer. We gave him the title of 'Goebbels'. Later that night a vicious brawl broke out in the bar area between Franco and anti-Franco factions. 'Goebbels' had a good view and would have been able to report another victory to his master, Franco, since all the anti-Franco faction were taken away in handcuffs by the police. He also met us at another small harbour on the North Coast of Spain and finally was waiting for us in La Coruna. Mick Hartnett insisted that he bring us to the Chief of Police in the town where he produced his United Nations identity card for UNFICYP in Cyprus. The police were highly embarrassed and apologetic for this misunderstanding and we were free to pursue the rest of our adventure.

Overseas Service

Paddy Walshe

In October 1963 I travelled to the Congo with the Artillery Section of the 2nd Inf. Group. This was an extraordinary experience. The OC, Lt Col Reddy O'Sullivan, appointed me as Assistant Welfare Officer to Capt Terry McKeever with responsibility for all valuable items (watches, golf clubs, cine cameras and about 100 other such items). That occupied most of my time in the Congo and was an extremely interesting and taxing appointment.

At one stage, Lt Harry Quirke and I were directed to do a patrol for several days in the direction of the Angolan border. We had a fully armed platoon and camped one night alongside the native Baluba village of Kazafu. We found the Balubas extremely helpful and friendly. They invited us to attend their nightly chanting, dancing and drumming session around their big campfire. The Balubas had a bad name at this time due to the Niemba ambush sometime previously. We agreed that they did not deserve such a reputation. For the remaining nights of the patrol, we slept on roadways.

Halfway through our Congo posting, Lt Martin O'Neill, of the Cav Sqn, and I were directed by the CO to drop leaflets along the Rhodesian border inviting armed rebels who were still located there to return to their nearest police station, hand in their weapons and be given an amnesty. We dropped thousands of leaflets over a very extensive area. As the helicopter was landing again in Kolwezi airport, some high pressure system in the transmission malfunctioned and the landing was fast and bumpy. The pilot told us that if it had happened half an hour earlier, we would still be somewhere on the Rhodesian border with very little way of getting back to Kolwezi.

Getting to the Congo was one of the highlights of my whole life.

Final Days of Army Life

Paddy Walshe

In early February 1980, as a senior instructor in the Artillery School, I was tasked with bringing a group of five young officers to Bofors at Karlskoga in Sweden to take over a new weapons system, RBS 70. The course lasted until the end of May. The RBS 70 is a laser-guided missile anti-aircraft system.

The most extensive part of the course was designed to make us qualified operators and aimers which proved to be very onerous. Eventually we all got the high qualification of Laser-Guided Trackers.

On return to Magee Barracks, Kildare, I established our own training section for this weapon. The weapon is still in use with the Artillery Corp., but now it has sophisticated radar assistance with the tracking process.

My army service finished with the posting as OC apprentice school Aer Corps. From there I retired from the Defence Forces on the 6th of February 1983, having completed 22 years' service.

Appreciation of the help given to me by other classmates

In particular I wish to thank Eugene Lavelle for his assistance with critical technical adjustments to some equipment in the years after I retired.

To George Kirwan, who due to his connections to security at the airports arranged for me to join the international press corps to cover the visit of Pope John Paul to Ireland in 1979. I got a place in the press pool of six photographers and a prime location on the photographers' stand overlooking the huge crowd in the Phoenix Park. I was the only photographer allowed on the tarmac at Shannon with the Pope. (Much to the chagrin of hundreds of other photographers present). And finally, George arranged with Áras an Uachtaráin that I put on a private exhibition of twenty photographs of the visit for President Hillery. This resulted in my panoramic picture of the million people in The Phoenix Park being selected by the President for installation on the concave wall in the Aras. It is framed in curved mahogany 20 feet wide. The job was completed with the assistance of craftsmen from the OPW in late 1982.

Credit also to John Martin and Des Travers who, with great effort, kept contacts within the 35th Cadet Class alive during all the intervening years.

To Mick Hartnett who was a great friend to me from the day I first met him at the Cadet Interviews and who advised me as I went into the interview room to "tell them anything you know about birds — they will love it".

Frank Cotter also was a great friend of mine, and we had adventures together, many of which were risky. I continued to keep in contact with Frank when he joined the Zambian Police Force in 1967 and visited him in April 1971 at his new family abode in Waterlooville near Portsmouth.

Finally, my dear friend from Castletownbere, Michael O'Sullivan; he was a regular caller to my photographic processing department for many years, as I printed the wonderful photographs he had taken of major civil engineering projects and large scale landscape photographs from all parts of the country. He was a dedicated professional. Michael still visits me whenever he is up from his hometown.

I have the greatest respect and admiration for all other members of our Cadet Class. Likewise, I found that the vast majority of Senior Officers in the army were honourable and decent people and were by and large very kind people. I have only fond memories of my time in the Cadet School and of my general military service up to the time of my retirement, which also included a posting to Cyprus with the 18th Infantry Group in 1970 where I first met my wife to be, Carmel.

Viking Excavations in Dublin

Lars Kempe, translated by Carmel Walshe

The City Library in Karlskoga requested Patrick Walshe from Kildare in Ireland to exhibit photographs that he has taken of the Viking site excavations at Wood Quay in Dublin. The National Museum of Ireland has the responsibility for supervising the excavations. Mr Walshe, who is visiting our city for a few weeks, had in his possession ten mounted photographs with details of the excavations. When our library historian discovered this he arranged for Mr Walshe to mount a formal exhibition of his pictures at the Library.

From October 1978 until December 1979 he took about a thousand pictures on the site. He will continue to do so when he returns from Sweden. All the photographs were taken with the assistance and the direction of the Museum archaeologists. This is the first time these pictures have been exhibited publicly. He is hoping to have a larger exhibition with about a hundred pictures later this year in Dublin, but the people of Karlskoga have become the first to see any of them.

The Viking site at Wood Quay was discovered in the early 1960s. Today many archaeologists are engaged in excavating the site. The Vikings arrived in Ireland around the year 840 AD but the location of their original settlement is not known. The site of the present excavations probably date from the year 950 AD.

In Ireland, interest in the Vikings has increased as the excavations progressed. Archaeologists have exposed a large portion of the Wood Quay settlement. Many parts are very well preserved. In Patrick Walshe's exhibition in Karlskoga library you can see the walls and doorways of houses. The perfectly preserved axe cuts in the wooden breakwater timbers are clearly visible. Also discovered were burials with three complete skeletons. Many skeletal parts of both humans and animals have also been discovered.

Patrick Walshe says his photography is a hobby, but it seems to be far more extensive than that considering the documentation he has done on this project.

Footnote:

Patrick Walshe was the only non-museum photographer permitted access to the Wood Quay site. He used some very specialised equipment to obtain the most dramatic pictures. He acknowledges the great assistance he got from the National Museum staff, in particular from Pat Wallace, the Excavation Director. The site was visible from the top of Christchurch Cathedral and Patrick Walshe was given permission by the authorities to take overall photographs of the site from the heights of the Cathedral. Patrick Walshe authorised the directors of the Karlskoga Library to allow other libraries throughout Sweden to exhibit the photographs if they so wished.

Vikingafynd i Dublin

KARLSKOGA. På biblioteket i Karlskoga ställer Irländaren Patrick Walshe från Kildare ut bilder från utgrävningarna av vikingastaden i Dublin, som sker i National Museum of Irelands regi.

Han är på ett par veckors besök i staden, och hade ett tio-tal fotografier med sig. På biblioteket fick man reda på detta, och ordnade snabbt en utställning.

Patrick Walshe har följt utgrävningarna intensivt under perioden oktober -78 mars -79 och tagit ca 1.500 bilder under tiden. Även efter mars -79 har han fortsatt sitt fotoarbete.

— Men huvuddelen av bilderna är tagna under den mest känsliga delen av arbetet och har ett stort arkeologiskt värde, säger han.

Foto som hobby

Patrick Walshe har fotografering som hobby, men det verkar vara en omfattande fritidssysselsättning med tanke på den dokumentation han har gjort enbart vid utgrävningarna.

— Det är första gången några av bilderna visas offentligt, sä-

ger han. I Dublin har jag planerat att göra en större utställning med ett 100-tal av fotografierna senare. Men Karlskoga blev först.

Vikingastaden upptäcktes i början av 60-talet, men det är först under senare år, som man satsat ordentligt på att ta fram boplatsen.

Ekonomiskt stöd

— Den irländska staten har givit projektet mycket stöd i form av pengar. I dag är ett 70-tal personer sysselsatta med att ta fram lämningarna efter vikingarna.

— De kom till Irland första gången omkring år 840, men var den boplatsen finns vet man inte. Den man nu håller på att gräva ut är troligtvis från 950. Och nu är man framme vid år 1000.

Intresset på Irland för vikingarna har ökat under de senaste åren allt eftersom utgrävningarna fortskridit. Arkeologerna har fått fram en stor del av vikingastaden. Och många delar är mycket välbevarade.

På bilderna kan man se re-

Patrick Walshe från Kildare på Irland ställer ut några av sina bilder från utgrävningarna av vikingastaden i Dublin på biblioteket i Karlskoga.

sterna av ett hus med väggar och dörröppning. Yxhuggen i vågbrytarna av trä finns också kvar. Man har också påträffat

några gravplatser med tre kompletta skelett. Dessutom har skelettdelar av både människor och djur hittats. LARS KEMPE

A Man for All Sports

Tony Whelan (1940–2008)

By John P. Whelan

Christopher Anthony Whelan, Tony to all, was born in Dublin in 1940, the eldest of four children. During his early years he showed great athletic prowess, earning the nickname of 'Breezer' among his peers. As he progressed into secondary school at Synge Street CBS his football and hurling skills allied with his athletic prowess were nurtured and developed. Tony was selected for the Dublin hurling and football teams culminating in winning an All Ireland medal with the Dublin minor football team in 1958. In the same year he was placed third in the Leinster Colleges' long jump and fourth in the half mile. On leaving school he worked for a year with the B&I shipping company, then decided to apply for a cadetship in both the Army and Aer Corps.

UN Photo UNTSO 1980–82 Golan heights serving with UNDOF 1982
Photo includes: Comdt Des Donagh, Lt Col Des Swan,
Brig Gen Casey and Comdt Tony Whelan.

He was successful in both interviews and selected the Aer Corps. During his time as a cadet, in the Aer Corps he was a member of the Aer Corps GAA team that won the Dublin Senior championships. Another member of the same team was Lieut. Mick Hipwell, later to become his brother-in-law. Unfortunately, Tony's flying wasn't on a par with his gaelic football prowess and he was posted to the Cadet School in the Curragh joining the 35th Cadet Class for its final year. During his army cadetship he was selected to play for the Kildare Junior Hurling team, winning another All Ireland medal. On this team were four other cadets Larry Kiely, Noel Kelly, Paddy Curley and Ailbe O'Sullivan. He was commissioned in 1962 and posted to the Cavalry Corps Depot in the Curragh serving first in the 1st Tank Squadron and thereafter holding a variety of Cavalry Corps appointments throughout his career.

Tony was one of the first of his class to serve overseas with the UN in the Congo. His UN service continued with duties in Cyprus, Lebanon, and UNTSO in the Middle East with his last trip as a Military Observer in Cambodia. His sporting career continued, this time rugby, where he was on the Curragh RFC team that won the Provincial Towns Cup. He also won a Kildare Senior Championship medal with his local team, Eadestown. Larry Coughlan of Cavalry and the Offaly GAA team was also a member of the winning team. On his retirement from team sport he devoted his time to golf and bridge. His whole family was involved in the military. His brother Stef was a member of the 37th Class. His sister Joan married Mick Hipwell, and his youngest sister Christine, married Dick Heaslip, a member of the 37th Class. Tony's son Paul was also awarded an Aer Corp cadetship, achieved his wings and later was a member of the famed Aer Corp aerobatics team. Tony's life was cut short at the age of 69. He was first a gentleman, loving husband to Mary, his family and many many friends, civilian and military.

Ar dheis Dé go raibh a anam.

Gá Gasced An 35á Rang

1961 - 2021

An 35ú Rang
Gá Gasceð
1961 - 2021

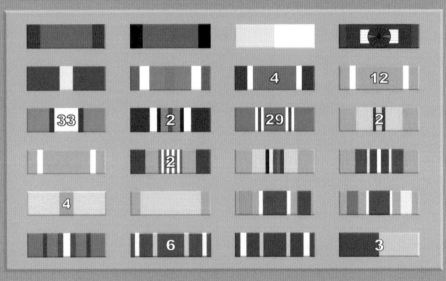

Scroll Index

(detail overleaf)

An 35á Rang
Gá Gasced
1961 - 2021

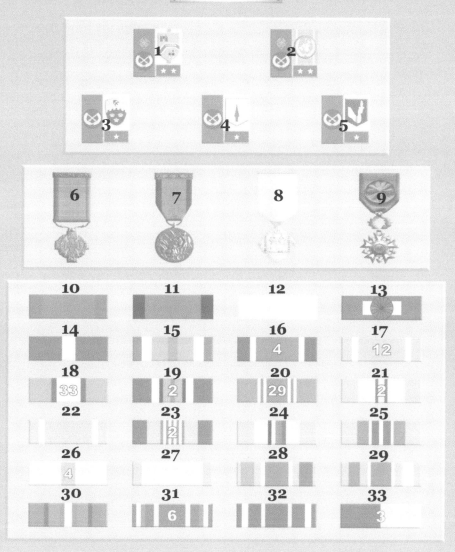

Scroll Reference

Service and Awards

This section provides a reference to the medals and ribbons displayed in the preceding scroll. Each featured medal is listed here in order of its number shown in the Scroll Index.

Note, for the ribbons (nos. 14–33) the number mounted centrally on the bar indicates missions carried out collectively by class members; e.g. the following indicates 29 UNIFIL missions served:

Commanding Generals

1. **Maj Gen John Vize**

   Force Commander, UNIKOM, Nov 1999–Nov 2001

2. **Maj Gen Carl Dodd**

   Chief of Staff, UNTSO, Mar 2002–Sep 2004

3. **Brig Gen David Taylor**

   GOC Southern Command, Sep 1998–Jan 2002

4. **Brig Gen Edmond Heskin**

   Assistant Chief of Staff, Oct 1997–Jun 1998

   GOC Eastern Command, Jun 1998–Oct 2003

5. **Brig Gen John Martin**

   GOC Western Command, Jul 1996–Oct 2001

Medals and Awards of Distinction

6 & 10. Comdt Michael Lynch

Military Medal for Gallantry with Distinction

Citation: For showing exemplary loyalty to his fallen United Nations Military Observers, and with disregard for his own safety, displaying the highest degree of courage and initiative in undertaking and successfully following through a difficult and dangerous mission, behind Syrian lines, in the mountains east of Beirut on the night of the 25th of September 1982, and for reflecting through his actions during the mission outstanding credit on himself and his country.

7 & 11. Comdt Joseph Fallon

Distinguished Service Medal with Distinction

Citation: As an observer (1973–1975) with UNTSO and subsequently as Force Commanders Personal Assistant and Military Assistant to Chief Coordinator of the UN Peacekeeping Missions in the Middle East, Commandant (then Captain) Fallon displayed dedication, initiative, leadership and resourcefulness well above the ordinary. Overall his contribution to UN peacekeeping in the Middle East was outstanding.

8 & 12. Comdt (Retd.) Joseph Fallon

Medal Pro Ecclesia et Pontifice — Gold

Citation: In recognition of his service to the Catholic Healthcare Commission and for his contribution to healthcare services in Ireland in the area of intellectual disability and the development of palliative care. 2012 May.

9 & 13. Maj Gen Carl Dodd

Commander, National Order of the Cedar (Lebanon)

For great services rendered to Lebanon, for acts of courage and devotion of great moral value, as for years in public service. 2006.

Service Medals

14.	Defence Forces Service Medal	
15.	Defence Forces Peacekeepers Medal	
16.	ONUC	— Democratic Republic of the Congo
17.	UNTSO	— Middle East
18.	UNFICYP	— Cyprus
19.	UNDOF	— Israel / Syria / Lebanon
20.	UNIFIL	— Lebanon
21.	UNEF	— Egypt / Israel
22.	UNGOMAP	— Afghanistan / Pakistan
23.	ONUCA	— Costa Rica / El Salvador / Guatemala / Honduras / Nicaragua
24.	UNTAG	— Namibia
25.	UNAMIC	— Cambodia
26.	UNIKOM	— Iraq / Kuwait
27.	MINURSO	— Morocco / Sahrawi Republic
28.	UNPROFOR	— Bosnia and Herzegovina / Croatia / Republic of Macedonia / FR Yugoslavia
29.	UNTAES	— Croatia
30.	UNTAC	— Cambodia
31.	ECMM	— Former Yugoslavia
32.	EUMM	— Former Yugoslavia
33.	OSCE	— Europe

Statistics

★ Class' cumulative military service: 891 years

★ Overseas: 89 years, representing 10% of total service

★ Service occurred across 30 regions in 4 continents, spanning a 42 year period

Timeline of Overseas Service

Bar colours correspond to ribbons detailed in scroll | UNGOMAP marked with ! to distinguish from UNTSO

UN: United Nations | PDF: Permanent Defence Force

Name	1963	1970	1975	1980	1985	1990	1995	2000	2005	Years served UN	PDF
Brownen, L.										5	42
Cooke, L.										3	40
Cotter, F.										1	10
Dodd, C.										6 ½	45
Draper, E.										½	10
Fallon, J.										4 ½	28 ¼
Hartnett, M.										2 ½	38
Hayes, W.										2	40
Heskin, E.										4	43
Jordan, K.										3	38
Keane, R.										½	38
Kiely, L.										1 ½	38
Kirwan, G.										3	20
Lynch, M.										3	38
Martin, J.										3	40 ¾
Murray, J.										8 ½	42
O'Murchu, P.										5 ½	38
Prendergast, J.										1	42
Sweeney, M.										4 ½	38
Taylor, D.										4	42
Travers, D.										5 ½	41 ¾
Vize, J.										5	43
Walshe, P.										1	22
Whelan, A.										4	40

All proceeds of this book go to the registered charity
Óglaigh Náisiúnta na hÉireann (ONE) which provides
Support, Comradeship, Advocacy and Remembrance (SCAR)
for Irish Veterans

Printed in Great Britain
by Amazon